Decorative Art

20 STEP-BY-STEP PAINTED FURNITURE PROJECTS

TAHIRA LEWIS

B.T. BATSFORD LTD

LONDON

DEDICATION
To Stephen, Jason and Natasha, my wonderful family, for all their sacrifices.

ACKNOWLEDGMENTS
I wish to thank all my friends, teachers and students for their help and
encouragement. With very special thanks to Phillip Chambers, Ann
Whitchell, Karen Gunnell and Farnosh Zahab for lightening the load,
and to Venetia Penfold for all her help and guidance. I couldn't have
had a better editor to tackle the difficult task of turning a painter into a writer.

First published in 1997 by
B. T. Batsford Ltd
583 Fulham Road
London SW6 5BY

A catalogue record for this book is available from the British Library.

ISBN 0 7134 7992 2

Printed in Hong Kong

Photography by Marie-Louise Avery
except page 68 which is by Shona Wood

Contents

INTRODUCTION   4

THE HISTORY OF
DECORATIVE ART   5

CHAPTER 1

Materials and Techniques

Materials   8
Paint   8
Brushes   8
Equipment   10

Techniques   12
Preparing surfaces   12
Design   13
Paint techniques   14
Paint effects   16
Colour   18
Brushstrokes   20

CHAPTER 2

Round Brush

Blue and white tulip table   38
Sunflower platter   42
Daisy chair   46
Rose magazine rack   48
Flowers on a wall clock   52
Cockerel plaque   56

CHAPTER 3

Flat Brush

Pansy hat box   60
Poppy bread bin   64
Lion book box   70
Scroll wastebin   72
Blackberry breadboard   74
Naïve clock   78
Nautical lap desk   82

CHAPTER 4

Classic Painting

Rose and tulip tray   88
Fruit basket on cabinet   92
Lace book box   96
Roses and ribbon chair   100
Spring flower mirror   104
French style wardrobe   110
Antique chest   114

DESIGN TEMPLATES   116
LIST OF SUPPLIERS   142
INDEX   143

Introduction

Change your life and pick up a brush and paint!

In this book, I would like to show those of you who think freehand painting is the prerogative of the chosen few how, with simple techniques, you can transform everyday items in your own home and create tomorrow's heirlooms.

Everyone is creative. All too often as children you were made to feel that you either had the 'gift' or you didn't. There is no doubt that some people are especially gifted artistically, just as some people are great writers or mathematicians. However, this doesn't mean that we should not be taught how to hold a pen, form letters, build words and compose sentences. That is exactly what learning decorative painting is all about; how to hold a brush, mix colour, load a brush, form the basic strokes and create designs. These are all techniques which can be learned.

Can't draw? I couldn't draw when I first started. All you really need is the ability to trace and after a few patterns you too will find that you are learning how to draw.

Don't be discouraged with your first attempts; just keep practising and in a surprisingly short time you will get there. Correcting mistakes is all part of discovering how to be creative and daring again. If you make mistakes, so what? Nothing is carved in stone. You can always sand it off, paint over it again or, like me, just hide it at the back of the garage until you are ready to face it again!

Remember that everyone's handwriting is different – so your painting will have its own unique style. Sometimes my students bemoan the fact that their work doesn't look like mine, but it would be a shame if it did, because it is good to let your own character and sense of colour express itself in your painting. It is exciting to see a range of styles and I am constantly delighted by my students' individual and original use of colour and technique. Don't take yourself or your painting too seriously; in Somerset Maugham's words,

Perfection has one big defect. It is apt to be dull.

The fact that decorative and folk art painting does not concern itself with realism allows for a wonderful spontaneity of expression. *Spontaneity* – remember that word every time you pick up a brush.

Once you have mastered the basics you will be able to refine the various techniques and projects shown in this book and take your painting to whatever level suits you.

The history of decorative art

The art of decorating your home environment is a tradition which dates back to prehistoric man. All cultures seem to have a deep need to enhance their surroundings and the decorative styles and range of artefacts produced throughout the history of mankind continue to influence our everyday life.

Painted furniture as we know it today has its roots in the seventeenth century. As trade with the Far East developed, the fashion for oriental painted furniture grew rapidly amongst the monarchy and aristocracy of Europe. The long process of creating lacquerware in China and Japan plus the protracted shipping times meant that orders often took years to complete. European cabinet makers, looking for ways to emulate these products in response to popular demand, created a style called Chinoiserie. The decorative painters in the eighteenth and nineteenth centuries added new styles and techniques to this fashion to meet the demands of their customers. This included the development of designs which interpreted the decorative styles of the Middle Ages and Renaissance.

In Northern and Eastern Europe, the demand for painted furniture filtered down from the aristocracy to the lower levels of society and was interpreted according to the population's means and needs. Perhaps it was due to the long hard winters that the tradition of women decorating their own household furnishings developed.

Folk Art in England developed along rather different lines and was mainly enjoyed by the aristocracy. In the eighteenth century, the architect, Robert Adam, inspired by the Italian example, designed furniture which was then decorated by professional artists such as Angelica Kauffmann in a style which reflected the architectural setting. Tole and pâpier maché of this period was mostly decorated in the factories where they were produced.

Travelling showmen were the first to decorate caravans in the eighteenth century, rather than the gypsies who didn't take to the roads until the late eighteenth century. The particular style of castles and roses used on the canal boats was probably brought to England by the Romany gypsies; the castles depicting the typically Eastern European onion-top roofs. The barges only started to be decorated as this method of transport went into decline. Consequently, the family was conscripted to supply cheap or free labour and as a result, the barges became their homes – hence the need for decoration.

Early American colonists in the seventeenth century were influenced by the decorative traditions of migrating Europeans. A new impetus for decorative painting came in the mid-eighteenth century when religious upheavals in Europe sent a flood of migrants to the new world from Germany, Holland, Switzerland, Silesia and Moravia. Many settled in Pennsylvania. The women took on this art form as part of their homemaking skills, infusing it with a wonderful vitality as they decorated virtually every object in the home.

We largely owe the current revival of Decorative and Folk Art painting to our cousins in America. It is interesting to note that a trade which was predominately the domain of men has been left to women to revive.

Chapter 1

MATERIALS AND TECHNIQUES

In this chapter you will learn how to master the practical skills required for the 20 stunning projects which follow. After a comprehensive list of materials, an illustrated step-by-step guide shows how to perform the variety of brushstrokes used throughout the book. In addition, there is a section on techniques for preparing surfaces plus different methods for creating a variety of backgrounds.

Materials

The huge range and high standard of paints, brushes and other materials available will give you the flexibility to create the exciting effects shown in this book.

PAINT

This book focuses on the use of acrylic paint as the most popular choice for decorative art. Acrylic paint is non-inflammable, non-toxic and flows easily while allowing the controlled application of the paint. It is not necessary to buy a great range of colours to get started.

I would recommend the following colour range for beginners: Yellow Oxide, Burnt Umber, Hooker's Green, Alizarin Crimson, Cobalt Blue, Titanium White, Antique White and Black. In order to broaden the range of colours available, you could add colours with basic pigments such as Cadmium Yellow, Cadmium Orange, Purple Dioxide and Turquoise. Ready-mixed colours also have their place, offering the convenience of having your favourite colours to hand.

I use my own brand of Tahira's Acrylic Paint but other brands available are Liquitex, Folk Art, Deco Art, Jo Sonja and Matisse. Most of the colours used for the projects in this book can be made up from half a dozen pure pigment colours. Traditional artists' colours form part of an international colour classification and are available with oil, watercolour or acrylic paints.

BRUSHES

There are different types of brushes suitable for decorative painting. Brushes made from Taklon are popular, inexpensive and easily available.

There are a large variety of brush shapes which have been specially designed to enable you to achieve effective strokes with ease. I would advise

you to start with the two standard shapes, a No. 4 round brush and a No. 6 flat brush. Each project gives individual details of the range of brushes required, so don't buy them until you have decided which projects to tackle. You can extend your range of brushes as your technique develops.

Round brush (No. 1, 2, 4, 6)

The ferrule of the round brush is cylindrical and this gives the brush its name (Fig. g on photograph). The hairs of the brush are shorter on the outer edges, increasing in length towards the centre so the brush head comes to a fine point. This is the traditional brush for stroke work but it can also be used for shading and blending.

Flat brush (No. 4, 6, 8, 12, 18)

Also called a shader brush, this has a flattened ferrule with the hairs cut straight across the top which is referred to as the chisel edge (Fig. h). These brushes are particularly good for shading and highlighting but are also used for stroke work. An angle shader is the same as a flat brush but the chisel edge is cut at an angle (Fig. c).

Deer foot stippler (No. 4, 6)

These are round brushes made with stiff hairs with the head cut at an angle (Fig. f). They are ideal for creating foliage or fur.

Glazing mop

These are round brushes with large, rounded heads like a make-up brush, also known as softening brushes (Fig. a). They are used on open paintwork to soften lines when antiquing or marbling. They should be used with retarder for acrylic paint and must be washed immediately after use.

Liner brush (No. 5/0)

Liner brushes are thin, round brushes with long hairs which act as an ink well for watered down paint, allowing you to pull long lines and swirls (Fig. i). They are ideal for outlining and veining.

Detail brush (No. 10/0)

This round brush has just a few short, fine hairs and is used for fine, detailed work (Fig. j).

Comb/Fan brush (1 cm/½ in.)

Also called a rake brush, this brush is thinned at the tip in a flat or fan shape. It is useful for painting grass, hair, fur and wood grain effects (Fig. d and Fig. b for comb and fan brush respectively).

Filbert brush (No. 6)

The filbert brush is the same as a flat brush, but the corners of the chisel end are rounded off, making the end an oval shape (Fig. e). When used for shading and blending they give a softer edge and are handy for creating quick petals and leaves.

Sponge brush (2 cm/1 in., 4 cm/1½ in., 7 cm/2¾ in.)

Also called a foam brush, this brush is a wedge of sponge with a little stiffening in the centre. It is used for background painting and reaches awkward corners. Make sure it is slightly dampened before use and squeeze the excess water out on an old towel.

Varnishing brush (4 cm/1½ in.)

This is a wide, flat Taklon brush with fine hairs to give a smooth finish. It is a worthwhile investment as finishing needs as much care as decoration.

Brush care

When using a dry brush, always soak it first thoroughly in water and wipe off excess on a tissue. Rinse your brushes regularly and make sure that you keep them immersed in water until you have time to clean them. Do not allow paint to build up in the ferrule while you are painting as this will make it difficult to produce good strokes. Brushes should not be left standing in jars of water as this will quickly damage the tip. Brush basins have the advantage of keeping the bristles immersed in the water while preventing the tip of the brush touching the bottom of the jar. When painting, treat your brush gently and do not scrub it round and round on the palette.

When you have finished painting, wash your brushes out in cold water with a little soap. Gently work the bristles around to make sure all the paint has come out of the ferrule. If paint is allowed to dry on the brush, it is hard to remove without damaging the bristles. After you have finished washing the brush, dab it on a tissue. If colour is still coming out then wash it again.

EQUIPMENT

A list of basic equipment is outlined below. Each project provides a list of materials, so don't buy everything until you see what you need.

Art carbon

Also called transfer paper, this wax-free, chalk-backed, carbon paper is used with tracing paper for transferring designs. It is available in various colours, so choose the colours according to the paints you are using so that the carbon colour does not show through. Do not use ordinary carbon paper, as the colour will bleed into the paintwork. Sometimes the art carbon marks can be a little stubborn to erase, in which case a tissue dampened with a little white spirit will quickly remove them without harming the paint.

Brown paper bags

Paper bags are excellent to use for smoothing edges and buffing surfaces.

Eraser

A good quality soft eraser is needed for removing any pattern lines left showing. This must be done before antiquing or varnishing.

Liquid masking

This is a rubber solution used as an adhesive in the carpet industry which has been repacked as liquid masking and is available through art shops. It is useful for masking off small surface areas. Apply with an old brush dampened with water and rinse it immediately. When applied to a smooth painted surface and left to dry it can be peeled off by rubbing with your finger.

Low tack tape

Low tack sticky tape is an alternative way of masking off an area while painting another. It is ideal for masking off large areas and creating straight lines.

Paint roller

A small sponge roller enables the easy application of background paint and varnish to large items. They give a slightly textured, even background.

Palette knife

This is useful for mixing larger quantities of paint rather than using your brush.

Palette

Acrylic paints dry permanently, so once left to dry, cannot be reused. Waxed paper or an old tile can be used or a wet palette which allows you to use the paint for longer. To make your own wet palette, wet a jaycloth, squeeze it out gently and wrap a sheet of greaseproof paper around it. Then lay it flat on a tile or in a shallow food container. The paint palette can be kept moist in an airtight box for quite a few days.

PVA glue

This is a water-soluble, plastic-based glue used for a variety of purposes. In these projects it is used to key the surface before painting.

Retarder

Retarder, also known as extender, is used to slow down the drying of paint and increase its flow. For detailed work the retarder is used on the brush or rubbed into the area to be painted. Always use it sparingly. First load the brush with the retarder, take off the excess by resting the brush on a paper towel until the sheen disappears and then load the brush with the paint.

Sandpaper

Use a fine to medium fine, wet and dry

sandpaper. Sanding blocks are good for large areas and emery boards are ideal for small, awkward places.

Shellac, sanding sealer and white polish

These are three methods of sealing wood and french polishing. They all dry very quickly and prevent resins from seeping out of the knots of new timber. They are not water-based so use methylated spirit as a thinner and for cleaning brushes. I like to use them for sealing as they give an excellent finish. They are very tough on brushes so keep a special one aside.

Cocktail stick sponge

This is useful when finely stippling very small areas, for example the centre of flowers (see page 68). Fix a small piece of a very fine marine sponge on a cocktail stick. First break off the point of the stick, drape the sponge over the top and tie it with a piece of cotton. It should look slightly bigger than a cotton bud.

Marine sponge

The varying sizes and shapes make them ideal for creating different stippled paint effects.

Make-up sponges

These are good quality fine foam sponges which can be cut up and used for painting the edges, legs and spindles of chairs. One of these sponges dipped into the paint spreads the paint smoothly and quickly. Remember to use a small brush first to touch in around the joints and spindles.

Steel wool

000 steel wool is good for distressing painted items by removing a thin layer of paint without causing scratch marks.

Stylus

This is a pointed, metal tool with a fine, ball head. It can be used instead of a pen for tracing and avoids a build-up of lines on the tracing if it is used several times. It is also ideal for creating lace effects and dotting in stamens. Create lines or swirls of graduated dots by dipping the stylus into the paint and starting a line of dots which will diminish as the paint runs out. For the same size dots, pick up the paint as you progress.

Tack cloth

This is a tacky cloth for removing specks of dust before painting. (A damp sponge is also good.)

Tracing paper

Semi-transparent paper for transferring patterns.

Water-based varnish

Water-based varnishes can only be used over water-based paints unless the oil-based paint is very old. Most are ideal for mixing with acrylic paints to make clear, coloured glazes. Matt varnishes should be stirred well before use. Brushes should be washed out in soapy water.

Oil-based varnish

Oil-based varnishes can be applied over acrylics as well as oil-based paints. It is important to stir both satin and matt varnishes from the bottom to the top as the settling out is more pronounced than acrylic varnishes. Brushes need to be cleaned first in white spirit and then washed thoroughly with soap and water. Wash several times until the soap foams.

Do not load your brush straight from the pot for either type of varnish, as this will contaminate the varnish with dust and fibres. Pour what you need into a dish and discard the remainder. You can use high gloss, satin or matt varnish according to your preference.

Techniques

The techniques which follow are essential to the overall finish of your project. You will learn how to prepare a variety of surfaces, create a range of paint effects and experience the excitement of developing brushstroke and painting skills – once thought to be out of reach.

PREPARING SURFACES

It is essential to prepare the surfaces properly as they must be an effective base for painting and decoration. Grease, rust, dirt and fingermarks will all affect the overall finish. The quality and colour of the surface must be planned at this stage in relation to the finished piece.

Glass/Enamel

Glass surfaces can be painted with most acrylic paints but purely for decorative purposes. For example, acrylic may come off in the dishwasher. There are other specialized glass paints available which will give extra protection and can be used in the same way as acrylic. Prepare the surface for painting by washing and rinsing with a solution of 1-part vinegar to 2-parts water.

Metal

Careful preparation of metal surfaces is essential, as rust which is not properly treated will break through the paint. Rust should be removed with a wire brush or steel wool and the area cleaned with a solution of 1-part vinegar to 2-parts water. Dry the piece immediately and, if possible, place it in a slightly warm oven overnight to dry out any residual moisture which will restart the rust process. Rust-inhibiting paint, available from hardware stores, should be applied at this stage. You could also get a large, rusty piece sandblasted and primed.

Terracotta

Only use new terracotta pots, as used pots have accumulated salts which will affect the paint finish. Paint the inside and outside of the pot with a mix of 1-part PVA to 2-parts water until it saturates the surface. Then leave it to dry. It is now ready for painting.

MDF board

This consists of very fine wood fibres bonded with glue. Good quality MDF does not need sanding or sealing as it already has a surface preparation, so you will only need to sand the cut or routed edges. Sanding the finished surface will expose the fibres which will swell with the moisture from the paint and cause unnecessary work. On some MDF, water-based paints may cause fibres to swell. If this happens, buff the board with a crumpled brown paper bag or sand lightly with fine sandpaper between coats.

Wood

Natural wood grains can make effective backgrounds. Fill any holes or gaps with a wood filler that matches the colour of wood that you are using. Create a smooth surface with fine sandpaper or, if the surface is already smooth, buff with a brown paper bag. Always sand in the direction of the grain, paying special attention to the edges and joints.

Painted, wooden items can be stripped or sanded. If the item is in reasonable condition, the surface can be smoothed and cleaned for repainting. Use touch as well as sight to feel any bumps when you are sanding. Sand until smooth and wipe over the surface with white spirit to remove any dirt and grease. Use a tack cloth or a damp, lint-free cloth to remove any dust before moving to the next stage.

Sealing

It is not necessary to seal MDF board or wood before using acrylic water-based paints. If you want to paint using the wood grain as a background, paint your design directly on the wood. You could also use shellac or clear varnish to protect the surface (see page 11).

Wood staining

Staining allows the wood grain to show through the surface decoration. If possible, test a small area of the wood that is hidden from view.

First give it one or two coats of clear, watered-down varnish to seal the grain and any joints. This will prevent the stain from being absorbed unevenly. When dry, lightly sand with a fine grade paper or buff with a brown paper bag. It is not necessary to buy ready-prepared wood stains, especially if the project is small. Add a little acrylic paint of the colour you require with a little water to a water-based varnish (approximately 1-part water to 4-parts varnish). You now have a stain that can be applied to a finished surface or directly to the wood.

Painting the basecoat

When applying a background colour, always use a good quality brush. Wet your brush before dipping it in the paint and wipe off the excess water. Two or three thin coats of paint are preferable to using one thick layer which may create ridges of paint. Apply the paint with long, even strokes. If you find the paint is drying before you have quite finished, pick up a little more water on the brush. When the first coat is dry, sand it lightly with fine sandpaper or buff with a paper bag. Make sure you always sand in the direction of the wood grain, then dust and repaint. When basecoating a large piece of MDF, I sometimes wipe it over with a damp cloth first. This stops the paint drying too quickly and gives it a very smooth finish. However, do not soak the MDF as it may make the fibres swell.

DESIGN

Once you have chosen your piece of furniture and prepared the surface, the next stage is to decide on the position of the design.

There are several methods to help you with layout and colour. You can lay the pattern on the item to be painted and stand back to see where you would like it to be positioned or trace and paint the design on a card painted in your chosen background colour. Alternatively the design can be painted on acetate or tracing paper, which you can lay on your project to see how it will look. You can also cut these up to rearrange the elements of the design.

Transferring a design

Firstly, trace the design. There are black-and-white design templates for each of the projects at the back of the book which can be traced from the page. These can be enlarged with a photocopier and adapted to suit other pieces of furniture.

Position the tracing on the surface, fix it with low tack tape and slide the transfer paper underneath, making sure that the active side is *facing down* (this is a common mistake!). You must slide the carbon under after the tracing paper has been placed to make sure that the pattern is in the correct position. Go over the outlines with a stylus, using enough pressure to leave the design on the surface. Don't press too hard or you will dent the wood.

The transferred lines are only an indication of where to paint. A sensitive or expressive stroke is always more effective than a 'filled in' look. Any lines left showing after painting should be erased.

PAINT TECHNIQUES

The techniques which follow show how to apply your newly learnt brushstrokes to create different effects with your painting.

Blocking in

Choose a brush size appropriate to the area that you are blocking in. Always start away from the edge of the outlines of the pattern. This way you won't get a ridge of paint building up where the two colours meet. Work towards the edges, using strokes that follow the shape of the area that you are blocking. By working slowly towards the line you will keep the definition of the line when painting the adjoining colour. If ridges of paint are formed as the paint squeezes out from the side of your loaded brush, it is too full. Wipe the excess off and run the brush back over the ridges to flatten and smooth them.

Cross hatching

Firstly to explain how you cross hatch with a long liner brush. The brush must travel smoothly across the surface, so load it well with paint, watered down to an inky consistency. Practise pulling the brush in lines towards you to build up a rhythmic stroke to produce an even series of lines. Turn the paper and repeat in the other direction to produce the cross hatching effect (see Lace book box on page 96).

An unusual background effect can be created using a flat brush. Pick up the base colour and a little white on a flat brush. Using short, random cutting strokes criss-cross the paint on to the background, alternating the strokes with lighter and darker shades of the background colour.

Dry brush

This technique can be used for highlighting or shading. Dip the brush in retarder and blot off the surplus moisture. Load the brush with paint and wipe it off on a tissue with a stroking motion until there is virtually nothing left on the brush. Lightly stroke the brush on to the surface and slowly build up the intensity of colour. Remember it is better to have too little paint on the brush than too much.

Fly specking

This technique of splashing dots of paint on a surface emulates the specks often seen on old paintings or furniture. Use a stipple brush or an old toothbrush. Mix a little Burnt Umber with some water to an inky consistency, dip the brush in this mix, tap off the excess moisture and using your nail, pull back along the bristles letting them flick the paint on to your project piece. Practise to see how much paint is coming off the bristles and how close the brush should be to the surface.

Push/pull technique

This technique is used for defining the edges of petals. For example, when painting a poppy petal using Orange Light as the primary colour and defining it with Alizarin Crimson. Using a round brush loaded with Orange Light and generously tip loaded with Alizarin Crimson, drizzle the Alizarin Crimson approximately 3-4 stroke widths along the edge of the petal or leaf to be painted. Then quickly wipe the excess Alizarin Crimson from the tip of the brush on a tissue.

Crimson from the tip of the brush on a tissue. The brush should still be full of the Orange Light. Now use comma strokes to fill in the petal. Start the comma just beneath the drizzled line of the Alizarin Crimson. Gently push the brush forward into the Alizarin Crimson so that the tip of the brush just catches a little and then pull back with the normal comma stroke. This should leave the ridge of paint but pull a little Alizarin Crimson down the petal.

Shading

There are two methods of shading. One is to use a darker colour or shade, side loaded on a clean, flat brush. This is blended on the palette by gradually walking the brush into the colour and back out again. The far edge must have absolutely no paint on it. This can be used around the edges of a petal to create a gradual increase in the intensity of colour on the edge fading away to nothing at the centre. The edge of the brush (side loaded with Burnt Umber) can be used below the outer edge of the petal to create a shadow. The second method for shading is to load first a flat brush with your main colour and then, on one side, load a darker shade of the main colour and blend them together on the palette. This creates a subtle blending of colour which is ideal for flesh tones, roses or leaves.

Tinting

This effect is achieved by watering down the colour you wish to use as a tint to a very thin wash. Load the brush with this wash then rest it on a tissue until the shine disappears. Stroke the colour lightly in the area, gradually building up the intensity of colour. If a little dot of water appears at the end of the stroke, the brush is too wet, in which case blot and try again.

Washes, glazing and floating colour

These techniques are used to overlay part or all of your project with a clear layer of colour through which the underlying work can be seen. They can also be used to shade under a flower or add subtle touches of highlight and shade to petals. The three methods are equally successful. I use all three, but tend to avoid using retarder as I like to work quickly and it takes a while to dry.

Washes

A wash is created by thinning paint down to various degrees of transparency with water.

Glazes

A glaze is paint thinned with a clear glazing medium, varnish or retarder to the required transparency - the same effect as floating colour.

Floating colour

This is the method of applying a transparent coat of paint by floating it on a surface which has been dampened with either a thin layer of water or retarder. This allows time to work the colour before it dries. Retarder keeps the paint workable for a longer period, but be careful to let it dry thoroughly before attempting a second coat. A side loaded flat brush is appropriate to float a transparent colour over this film. This is a good method to use on large areas where more than one stroke may be needed as it gives more time for blending out brushmarks. Floating is a skill which needs practice, but is an effective technique and worth developing.

Mistakes

There are ways of rescuing mistakes with paint. If you see immediately that you have made a mistake, a damp cloth or baby wipe will remove it. If it has dried, a little methylated spirits or alcohol on a cotton bud should remove the paint – however, beware not to damage the background paint. Leave to dry and paint over.

PAINT EFFECTS

When experimenting with the paint effects which follow, make up a large card for each effect with strips of your favourite background colours. Then apply the effects across them. This will give you an instant reference of colour variations for each paint effect.

Sponging

Natural sea sponges are excellent for this technique; they are much softer than manufactured ones, and have an irregular structure. Different sponges will give you a variety of effects according to their size and texture. Effects also depend on how hard you press the sponge on your project. You can gently pat the sponge up and down on the area for a fine, stippled effect, or slightly roll your wrist as you press down on to the project piece which can be striking when used with a marble mix, as it pushes the colours into each other. To keep your marine sponge in good condition, always wet it and squeeze it out before dipping it into any paint. Wash it out as soon as you have finished to keep it in good condition.

A simple masking method when sponging is to cut a piece of paper in the shape to be masked off, spray with removable mounting and fix in position. Do not soak the paper as this is a temporary measure.

Stippling

Stippling is a method of patting paint on to an area to give a soft, fuzzy look and it can be used as a background. Deer foot stippler brushes, small marine sponges or an artists' oil brush chopped off at the end are all good for this purpose. Load your brush or sponge with a watery mix of paint and pat the excess off on a piece of paper until the sponge or brush gives a speckled effect. You will then have the right amount of paint to start work (see Cockerel plaque on page 56).

Antiquing

This is a finishing effect combined with a colour which gives the surface an antique look. Before starting this process, make sure that the paint is completely dry. If it is cool to touch there will be remaining moisture. A hair-dryer can speed the drying process, but be careful not to burn your work by holding it too close. Make sure that all remaining chalk lines have been erased from your project. Instructions for mixing the antiquing medium are as follows:

1 Use 3-parts white spirit to 1-part raw linseed oil. Make up a reasonable amount of this antiquing medium in a jar as it can be put aside for future use. This can be used with any artists' oil paint colour, but Burnt Umber traditionally creates the impression of yellowing with age.

2 Squeeze out an inch of your Burnt Umber artists' oil paint on a small dish. Add some of the medium and mix to a soft, creamy paste.

3 Use a soft, lint-free cloth (old T-shirt fabric is ideal) or a brush and spread this mix over your project. **Don't panic** as the painting disappears! The linseed oil keeps the solution workable, giving you time to achieve the right look. Just keep going, making sure that you push the antiquing mix into any corners. Actual antique objects are always darker in the corners and grooves where dust, waxing and cleaning has

built up over time.

4 Using a soft, lint-free cloth, start to buff off the excess paint. Work from the centre with an even, circular motion, releasing the pressure as you work out towards the edge. Keep buffing until you are satisfied with the effect. Finally use a soft glazing mop or a soft make-up brush to gently buff over your work to soften it and to make sure that there are no smears. Be careful not to finger it while it is still wet as you will leave finger-marks. (If you don't like the effect, wipe it off with a little white spirit on a cloth.)

Put it to one side to dry for a week to 10 days. Varnish it with either a polyurethane or water-based varnish. An oil-based varnish may be used after two days (see page 38).

Important The products used for antiquing are highly inflammable. Keep away from direct heat and dampen the cloths before disposal.

Crackle glaze

I hope to dispel the confusion regarding the two different techniques of crackling. The glaze is used when applying a background finish. It is sandwiched between two coats of paint, preferably different colours so the effect is accentuated. To give an example, paint the surface of a card Terracotta, let it dry and then coat with the clear crackle glaze. Once the crackle glaze is dry, paint the whole of the card with your second colour, for example Antique Blue. Ensure that the paint is applied quickly and evenly. Never sweep back over an area twice as the crackling reaction starts as soon as the paint touches the glaze. (If you sweep the brush back again before the paint has dried you will disturb the reaction; the result will be no cracks and a lumpy mess which you will have to wipe off quickly with a damp cloth.) Leave it to dry before touching any areas that have been missed.

Another method of application is to apply the top coat of paint with a marine sponge which gives a nice crazed effect. Thinning the top coat of paint with a little water makes its application easier both with the brush and the sponge. The thicker the paint, the larger the cracks. Enjoy experimenting with both techniques on sample cards. Your design may also craze as you paint over these effects.

Crackle varnish

This type of crackle is used to create a cracked effect over your final painting. Crackle varnish comes in a two-part pack. The first part is oil-based and the second is water-based.

Apply the first part of the oil-based crackle varnish evenly over the whole surface of your decorated item. Some solutions can be quite viscous, so adding a little white spirit to the brush will thin it and make it easier to spread evenly. Allow this surface to 'come to tack'. This means it is almost dry, but feels slightly tacky when pressed firmly with your finger. The brush should be cleaned out with white spirit.

Then apply the water-based second part of the crackle varnish evenly over the whole surface. This can be diluted with a little water if you find it hard to spread. The thicker the varnish, the larger the cracks. Make sure you have left no gaps in this layer as this will mean that the surface will not crack evenly. Now leave it to dry thoroughly for approximately 2-3 hours. The drying time will depend on the air humidity and can be aided by putting the piece in an oven that has been turned off and is nearly cold. Then use a hair-dryer to increase the crazing effect.

The fine cracks are hard to see at this stage unless you hold the item up to the light. All the

cracks become apparent after applying the antiquing mix over the entire surface. Leave for a few seconds and buff off as required. The antiquing medium will also stop the cracks from disappearing with moisture from the air on damp days. Finish off with a coat of oil-based varnish which must be applied to protect the surface.
If at any stage you are unhappy with the surface, it can be wiped off (the first coat with white spirit and the second coat with water). (Please see Blue and white tulip table on page 38.)

Marble mix

A marble mix is made up of 2-3 colours drizzled randomly on to a palette and then lightly stirred to create a marbled effect. This can then be used with a brush or a sponge.

White marble

Paint the background Antique White. Then mix a dash of Payne's Grey with approximately 3-parts Antique White to 1-part water and 2-parts varnish plus a few drops of retarder. Paint the surface with this mix and then quickly lay a plastic bag over the wash and lift it off, which will create a veined look. With a damp cloth wipe out random patches. Add a little more Payne's Grey to the mix and accentuate some of the shapes and veins left by the plastic with a feather. (Please see Fruit basket on cabinet on page 95.)

COLOUR

There is no need to feel daunted by using colour. There are many books devoted to the theory of colour which you might like to look at. However, experiment and practice are the most direct ways of learning to use colour effectively. Although the instructions for the projects follow the exact colour scheme used for each project, they can be easily adapted to your individual preference.

The simple chart on page 19 gives a guide to mixing a selection of colours from a small range of basic colour pigments. I hope that this will encourage you to create colours of your choice. The colour amounts shown for each of the recipes give approximate proportions of each colour to be mixed. While mixing the colour you require, you will soon see how the various pigments affect each other according to the proportions used. If you were mixing blue with Alizarin Crimson you would get a very dark purple, but by adding increasing amounts of white you will go through all the shades of purple, down to a very pale lilac. You will see how yellow, rather than white, can be used to lighten the depth of Hooker's Green. When mixing Alizarin Crimson and white to make pink, a touch of Yellow Oxide will change bright pink into a subtle, dusty pink. Black can be used to darken Cobalt Blue and Hooker's Green. However, when added to red, the resulting colour is brown.

Choosing colour

Choosing a main background colour can sometimes be difficult. When deciding which colour to paint your project, consider your colour preferences, the colours in the room where the project will be situated and the style of the project itself. By painting cards in various colours, you will be able to judge which scheme you prefer. Trace your pattern on to the card and check the colours on the different backgrounds. (Cut up old cereal packets for test cards.) If you are a beginner, I would advise keeping to plain backgrounds which can be touched up easily if mistakes are made. It is more difficult to match or touch up a paint effect background.

Colour recipes

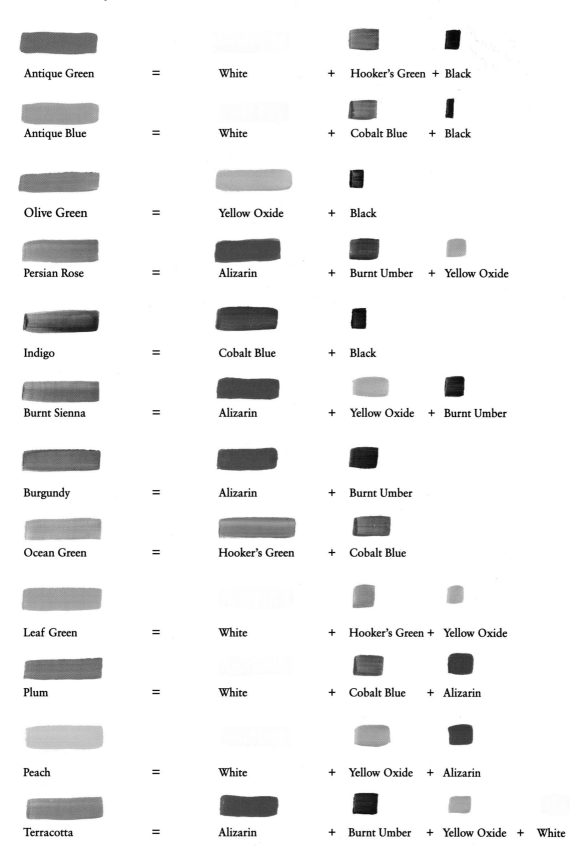

Antique Green = White + Hooker's Green + Black

Antique Blue = White + Cobalt Blue + Black

Olive Green = Yellow Oxide + Black

Persian Rose = Alizarin + Burnt Umber + Yellow Oxide

Indigo = Cobalt Blue + Black

Burnt Sienna = Alizarin + Yellow Oxide + Burnt Umber

Burgundy = Alizarin + Burnt Umber

Ocean Green = Hooker's Green + Cobalt Blue

Leaf Green = White + Hooker's Green + Yellow Oxide

Plum = White + Cobalt Blue + Alizarin

Peach = White + Yellow Oxide + Alizarin

Terracotta = Alizarin + Burnt Umber + Yellow Oxide + White

BRUSHSTROKES

In this section, step-by-step photographs and instructions demonstrate how to hold and load the brush in order to perform a variety of strokes. The simple comma and 'S' strokes are the basic foundation of decorative and folk painting. With practice, these newly acquired skills will soon become second nature.

Setting up

You will need water, paper, a wet palette, paint brush and paper towels. The table should be a couple of inches lower than your elbow when you are seated.

Holding the brush

Rest the outside edge of your painting hand on the table and hold the brush between your thumb and forefinger at the point where the ferrule meets the brush handle. (The ferrule is the metal tube that holds the bristles.)

When painting, keep the brush at 90 degrees to the paper. You can control the paint more easily if you work slowly and with care. Relax and remember that any mistakes you make are not unique; every other painter, including myself has made them too!

A brushstroke practice sheet is included on page 141; remember that *practice makes perfect*! Lay a sheet of copy paper over the top and you will be able to use the strokes underneath as guidelines for practising your stroke work. Do not be afraid to move your work around to make it more comfortable for you to execute the strokes.

Round brush load

Having wet the brush, dab off the excess moisture on the brush and handle, especially any water that might be on the ferrule, as it will run down while you are painting and spoil your work. Don't overload the brush, but fill it with a manageable quantity of paint almost reaching the ferrule. Now you are ready to try the following strokes. If you have any problems, look at the visual guide to mistakes at the end of this chapter on page 29.

Round brushstrokes

The size of the stroke will be determined by the size of the brush and how much pressure is used. The paint must flow freely with a continuous movement. If you find that your strokes are a little heavy-handed when you first start to paint, try compensating for this by using a brush one size smaller. **Slow down!** Practise the strokes with slow, even movements. Speed comes with confidence as you develop an ability to control the brush and paint.

Comma stroke

1 Load your brush and keeping it erect, position it over the centre of the stroke and use your fingers to extend the brush to the top of the stroke. Then lay the bristles down and press so that they spread.

2 Use your fingers to gently draw the brush in a curving motion towards you while at the same time lifting the hand from the wrist to release the pressure from the brush. This allows the bristles to come back to a fine point.

'S' stroke

1 Load your brush making sure that you draw the bristles to a point on your pallet. Position it over the centre of the stroke, then extend it past the tip. Now pull it towards you, allowing the tip to glide down and gently touch the paper. As you pull your brush round, start to press down to widen the stroke.

2 At the middle of the 'S', start to lift as you come towards the tail, leaving the end of the stroke in a fine point (see Blue and white tulip table on page 38).

Exclamation stroke

1 Position the brush over the centre of the stroke, then use your fingers to extend the brush to the top of the stroke.

2 Lay the bristles down and press to make them spread. Gradually lift the brush while drawing it towards you.

3 Allow the brush to slightly roll between your thumb and forefinger which draws the bristles back to a fine point.

'C' stroke

1 Load your brush and make sure that you draw the bristles to a point on your palette. Position your brush over the paper, glide into the top of the 'C' stroke and apply pressure as you come down the back of the 'C'.

2 Lift off as you curve round to the tail. Work towards getting the top and tail the same. When the paint is side loaded on to the brush, this stroke is excellent for shading the centres and bases of roses (see Rose and tulip tray on page 90).

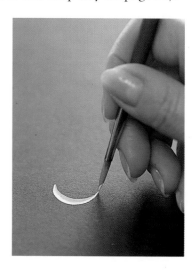

Liner brush loading

The long bristles on a liner brush act as an ink well. In order to load the brush you must thin the paint with water to an inky consistency. If the brush does not travel smoothly it is probably too dry, so add a little more water. If you add too much water, the paint will bleed across the surface.

1 Once loaded, the brush should be held in the usual vertical position to execute any fine strokes or lines. Only the tip of the brush is used and no pressure is applied (see Scroll wastebin on page 72). If you need to create long straight lines, glue a cork to each end of a ruler. This will raise it high enough for the liner brush to rest against the ruler.

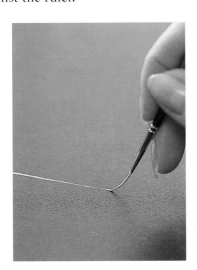

Wave stroke

1 The motion for this stroke is pressure and release. When you are putting pressure on the brush, the handle should tilt in the opposite direction of the waves. This forces the bristles to splay out to one side of the brush rather than evenly on either side.

2 Continue using a pressure and release action. Practise the regular shapes as shown here – but once you are more confident, you can vary the shapes.

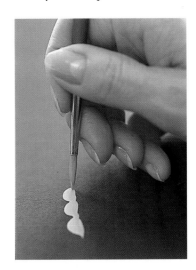

Fan stroke

1 Begin with a small comma. Position the brush as you would for a comma but do not pull the brush towards you.

2 Slightly roll the brush between your thumb and forefinger, forcing the bristles to fan out to one side.

3 When the fan is large enough, stop and gently lift the brush, without pulling, allowing the bristles to spring back to the base of the stroke.

Round brush loading

Having mastered the basic strokes you can now start to experiment with the various loading techniques which will give a greater depth and vitality to your work.

Tip load

Tip loading means picking up a small amount of paint on the tip of the brush. This can be done on a clean brush but is mostly used to add a second colour.

1 Load the brush with your main colour and pick up a small amount of a second colour on the tip of the brush (see Daisy chair on page 46). As you practise strokes with this loading technique you will soon start to see for yourself just how much colour is required.

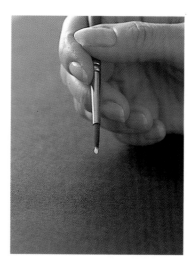

Side tip load

1 Load the brush with your main colour.

2 Holding the brush at a 45 degree angle
pull the tip lightly across the surface of
your second colour. Only a small amount
of the second colour is required. This
loading technique is ideal for creating leaf
and petal curls in conjunction with the
wave stroke.

Back load

1 Load the brush with your main colour and
pick up the second colour by resting the tip
of the brush next to this colour and
pressing the brush down so that it bends,
pushing the back of the brush into the
paint.

This loading technique can be used for
patting in the centres of flowers.

Kick load

1 This is an old method used in porcelain painting. Load the brush with your main colour and position it in the air behind your second colour.

2 Swing your brush forward so that the tip kicks the edge of the paint and picks it up on the topside of the brush tip. This loading technique can be used to create a highlight to one side of the small forget-me-not petals (see Rose magazine rack on page 50).

Flatten and side load

1 Load the brush with your main colour and lay the bristles of the brush on the palette. Using a zig-zag motion, walk the brush backwards out of the paint and turn the brush over and repeat. This will push out the excess paint and allow the brush to flatten. Banging the brush up and down on the ferrule will just ruin it. If it won't flatten, you may have too much paint or water on the brush – in which case wipe your brush and repeat.

2 Once the brush is flat, hold it parallel to the palette and gently pull the edge of the brush across the surface of the second colour. Now you should have a thin line of your second colour along one edge of your brush. Be careful not to lift the brush till the tip has completely cleared the paint. The technique is used to add another colour along the edges of strokes. The flattened brush can also be loaded with a third colour on the opposite edge which is called flatten and triple load (see Rose magazine rack on page 48).

Flat brushstrokes

Many of the strokes which you have learnt using a round brush can also be performed with the flat brush. In this book, the flat brush is used mostly for shading and blending. One or two colours are blended on the brush by stroking it up and down on the palette. I have included some stroke work with a blended brush using the ruffle technique. With two or three colours blended on the brush, the zig-zag movement creates effective striations of colour on petals and leaves. The ruffle stroke illustrated here is the half section of the leaf used on the Pansy hat box on page 60.

Ruffle stroke

1 Start the stroke with the flat brush standing on its chisel edge in a vertical position.

2 As you begin the zig-zag motion, allow the brush to roll between your thumb and forefinger, gradually swinging the chisel edge round to a horizontal position, adding pressure as you go. Walk the brush down the paper in a zig-zag motion which should come from the wrist.

3 Towards the end of the stroke, start to release the pressure until you are back on the chisel edge and roll the brush into the vertical position.

Side load

1 Pick the paint up on the corner of a damp, flat brush and stroke the brush back and forth on the palette, walking the brush halfway into the colour and back out.

2 It is very important not to take the paint all the way across the brush. The colour must blend away to nothing. This loading technique is useful for shading and highlighting (see Pansy hat box on page 60) and is ideal for shading the centres and bases of roses using the 'C' stroke (see page 22).

Double side load

1 This means side loading two colours on to one side of the flat brush. Pick up your first colour on one edge of the brush and blend on the palette until the colour is half-way across.

2 Pick up the second colour on the same side and blend again. You should now have two colours fading into nothing on the far side of the brush. This could be used as an alternative method to intensify the shading on the scroll on the Poppy bread bin on page 64. You can also add two other colours on one side to a brush that is already loaded with paint.

Triple load and blend

1 It is possible to load a flat brush with three colours. The brush starts off with one colour loaded all the way across and is then side loaded with a different colour on each edge.

2 This should then be blended on the palette ensuring that the brush is not overloaded (see Pansy hat box on page 60).

Brushstroke mistakes

The tail has been painted too rapidly, leaving no time for the paint to travel down the bristles of the brush. A little more water added to the paint will make it flow more easily.

The brush was set down at the wrong angle instead of in the direction of the stroke.

The brush has moved away from the beginning of the stroke before pressure was applied to open the bristles.

The brush was pushed right down to the ferrule which has left a mark. Then it was lifted off too suddenly and lost control of the comma.

The stroke was started too heavily. The brush should glide on the paper to the tip of the stroke which should be painted with light pressure.

Not enough pressure was applied in the middle of the stroke and the curves should be more gentle.

This stroke was done too hastily and the pressure sustained on the brush for too long, causing an uncontrolled shape.

The brush is tilting to one side, forcing the stroke to bulge more to the opposite side.

The flower and border directories which follow show how brushstrokes, loading techniques and colour can be used.

Chapter 2

ROUND BRUSH

This chapter concentrates on the basic strokes traditionally used for decorative painting. A variety of projects have been designed incorporating these simple techniques to gradually build up your decorative painting skills. Combined with the range of paint effect backgrounds, these simple brushstroke designs will allow you to give a new lease of life to furniture or wooden blanks.

Blue and white tulip table

This simple but effective design is an ideal project for beginners. Remember that simple designs can be just as successful as more intricate work. I have used crackle varnish and antiquing paint effects, but the design would look equally striking with fresh paint colours.

MATERIALS

Round brush No. 6

5 cm/2 in. sponge brush

5 cm/2 in. household paint brush

Varnishing brush

Soft make-up brush

Art carbon

Low tack tape

Stylus

Tracing paper

Hair-dryer

Antiquing medium

Crackle varnish

Oil-based varnish

Colour palette

Antique White

Antique Blue

Payne's Grey artists' oil paint

INSTRUCTIONS

1 Background Using a 5 cm/2 in. sponge brush paint the surface of the table and base with 2-3 coats of Antique White.

2 Trace the pattern Position and fix your traced pattern on the table with the tape. Slide the carbon underneath, making sure that the carbon side is facing down. Using the stylus, trace the outlines using enough pressure to leave the design on the surface without denting the wood.

3 Tulips Load the No. 6 brush with Antique Blue and tip load this with Antique White. Using the Comma and 'S' strokes paint in the tulips and leaves (see the worksheet on page 41 for the build up of the design). Once the paint is dry, erase any visible pattern lines.

4 Crackle varnish Using the household paint brush apply an even coat of the oil-based first stage of the crackle varnish over the whole surface of the table top and base. Leave to dry until it feels slightly tacky when you press your finger quite hard on the surface. Then give it the second water-based coat (see page 17).

As this is difficult to see, go over the surface in one direction (i.e. up and down) and then in the opposite direction (i.e. back and forth). It is important to make sure that you have covered the entire oil-based first coat. Any patches which are missed at this stage will become flat, brown patches when you antique the surface. The size of the cracks depends on how thickly you apply this second coat but be careful as too much will cause wrinkles.

5 **Antiquing** After leaving this to dry for two to three hours, apply direct heat to the surface with a hair-dryer which will encourage the surface to craze. To stabilise the crackles and heighten the crazing effect, antique the table top (see page 16 for full instructions). As the project is a blue colour, use Payne's Grey instead of Burnt Umber with the antiquing medium. Using a soft, lint-free cloth, spread your antique mix over the surface.

Start to buff off the excess using a soft, lint-free cloth. Use a circular motion, releasing the pressure as you work out towards the edge.

Buff over the surface with a soft glazing mop to make sure that there are no smears. If little stars of excess antiquing mix appear

where a few lines cross, remove with a cotton bud moistened with white spirit.

6 **Sealing** Seal the surface of the table with an oil-based varnish. This is very important as a water-based varnish will dissolve the crackle glaze. An alternative is to leave the piece for 7-10 days and wipe off the water-based glaze, leaving behind the fine lines of the Payne's Grey antique mix. Finally, apply the varnish.

Tip Practise crackle varnishing and antiquing on colour cards until you are confident you can achieve the finishes you require.

The two outer petals are 'S' strokes with their tails extended to meet at the base.

The centre petal consists of two comma strokes and an exclamation stroke overlapping each other.

Sunflower platter

These bold sunflowers are another good exercise for beginners. The size of the project will allow those of you who are just starting out to really go to town with lots of flamboyant 'S' strokes. Try to freehand the second layer of petals as it is just a matter of popping in random 'S' strokes over the first layer.

MATERIALS

Round brush No. 6

Deer foot stippler No. 6

7 cm/3 in. foam brush

Varnishing brush

Marine sponge

Art carbon

Chalk pencil

Low tack tape

Damp cloth

Retarder

Stylus

Tracing paper

Water spray or atomizer

Satin varnish

Colour palette

Russian Blue

Cerulean Blue

Antique White

Pale Lavender

Cobalt Blue

Hooker's Green

Burnt Umber

Cadmium Orange

Cadmium Yellow

Yellow Oxide

Yellow Light

INSTRUCTIONS

1 **Basecoat** Paint the platter with 1-2 coats of Russian Blue using the foam brush.

2 Using a damp cloth, wipe a thin film of retarder or water over the whole surface.

3 Dip a thoroughly dampened marine sponge into a marble mix of Cerulean Blue, Cobalt Blue and Pale Lavender. Work the colours into the sponge and quickly apply to the surface.

Before the paint dries, use a water spray to moisten the platter until the colours begin to run.

4 When dry, give it one thin coat of satin varnish.

5 Transfer the pattern

6 Leaves Block in the background of the leaves with a mix of Hooker's Green and Yellow Oxide on a No. 6 round brush. When this has dried, use a chalk pencil to indicate the centre of the leaf. Load the brush with Hooker's Green, tip loaded with Yellow Oxide. Using comma strokes, start from the base of the centre of the leaf and pull the commas out over the edge of the blocked-in leaves. Use a little more Yellow Oxide on one side of the leaf to indicate light coming from one side.

7 Sunflowers Load the round brush with Yellow Oxide mixed with a little Cadmium Orange and tip loaded with Antique White and paint the background petals with 'S' strokes. Paint the top layer of petals freehand with Yellow Oxide, mixed with Yellow Light and tip loaded with Antique White. Do not paint in the petals that overlap the centre at this point.

8 Using the deer foot stippler, stipple the centre of the sunflowers with Burnt Umber so that it just overlaps the base of the petals. With a little Yellow Oxide on the front tip of the deer foot stippler, define the inner part of the centre circle. A small amount of Hooker's Green can be stippled into the centre of the flower.

9 Load the No. 6 round brush with the mix of Yellow Oxide and Cadmium Yellow and tip load with White, then add the small petals that curl over the centres.

10 Finishing Give the platter 2-3 coats of satin varnish.

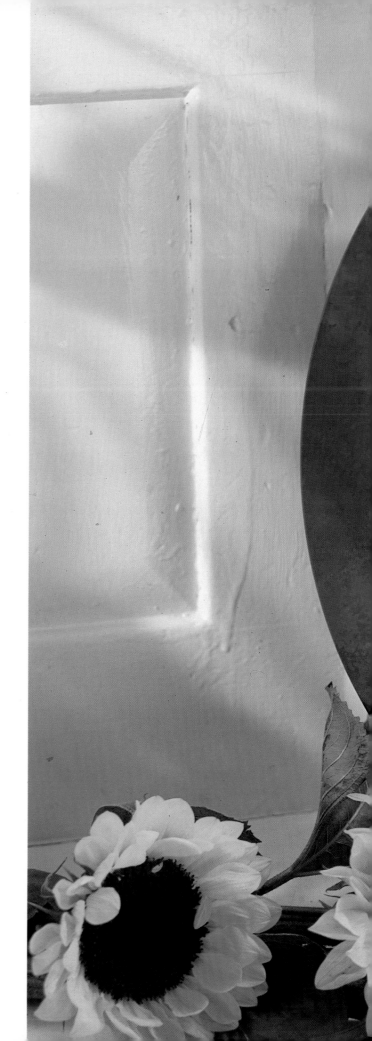

Daisy chair

This chair was inspired by a picture of Monet's kitchen in Giverny which showed the vibrant yellow and blue painted furniture glowing magically in the warm sunlight.

MATERIALS

Round brush No. 4

Make-up sponge

Varnishing brush

Art carbon

Fine sandpaper/brown paper bag

Low tack tape

Stylus

Tracing paper

Satin varnish

Colour palette

Parisian Yellow

Ultramarine Blue

Antique White

the sponge astride the corner, draw it straight along the edge in one swift movement.

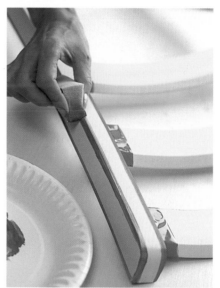

INSTRUCTIONS

1 **Background** Use a small brush to touch in the paint around the joints and spindles before using a make-up sponge to colour the whole background Parisian Yellow. Make-up sponges are ideal for this as they spread the paint very smoothly and easily on chair legs and spindles. Once the chair is dry, sand the surface with a fine sandpaper or buff with a brown paper bag before applying a second coat.

2 Mask the areas where the cross bands meet the back joints of the chair. Apply the lines of the blue border to the chair back and legs by dipping a small wedge of make-up sponge into a pale mix of Ultramarine Blue and Antique White. Dab off excess paint and then, placing

3 Transfer the pattern to the chair.

4 **Daisies** Use a pale mix of Ultramarine Blue and Antique White, tip loaded with Antique White on a No. 4 round brush. Use the comma stroke technique to paint in the daisies (see page 31) and scrolls on the chair sides and back. When the paint is dry, use a soft eraser to clean off any remaining traced lines.

5 Seal your work with 2-3 coats of satin varnish which can also be applied with a make-up sponge.

Rose magazine rack

The design on this magazine rack was inspired by the garlands of roses and tulips which are characteristic of Regency painted furniture. I have created this project using simple comma and 'S' strokes to show just how effective they can be. These elements combine to create a sophisticated and striking design.

MATERIALS

Round brush No. 4

Marine sponge

7 cm/3 in. sponge brush

Varnishing brush

Art carbon

Low tack tape

Stylus

Tracing paper

Crackle glaze

Satin varnish

Colour palette

Antique White

Antique Green

Hooker's Green

Yellow Oxide

Ultramarine Blue

Plum

Persian Rose

INSTRUCTIONS

1 **Basecoat** Using the sponge brush paint the magazine rack with pale Antique Green.

2 Use the design template to mark the area you wish to crackle glaze.

3 Paint the area under the garlands with the crackle glaze and leave to dry. Combine some Antique White into a wash with 2-parts water and 1-part satin varnish. Work the wash into a damp marine sponge on the palette. With a rolling movement cover the crackle glaze with this mix. Be careful not to go over the same area twice, for as soon as the paint comes into contact with the crackle glaze the chemical reaction will start. If you make a mistake, wipe the surface off with a damp cloth and leave to dry before starting again (see page 18).

4 **Transfer the design** Having ensured that the surface is completely dry, the next stage is to trace the flower pattern on to the magazine rack.

5 **Leaves** Mix a pale green colour using Hooker's Green, Yellow Oxide and Antique White. Load the No. 4 round brush and use the 'S' stroke to form the rose leaves and highlight them with Antique White. A paler version of this green, tip loaded with Antique White can be used for the small leaves which are just small, fat 'S' strokes. Add more White as you work towards the tips of the garlands which will give the impression that the leaves are fading into the background.

6 **Roses** Mix a pale pink with Persian Rose and Antique White. Load the No. 4 brush with pink, then flatten and side load with Antique White on one side and Persian Rose on the other. Paint in the three back petals using little half comma strokes. Dab the centres of the roses with a brush loaded with Yellow Oxide, back loaded with Persian Rose and tip loaded

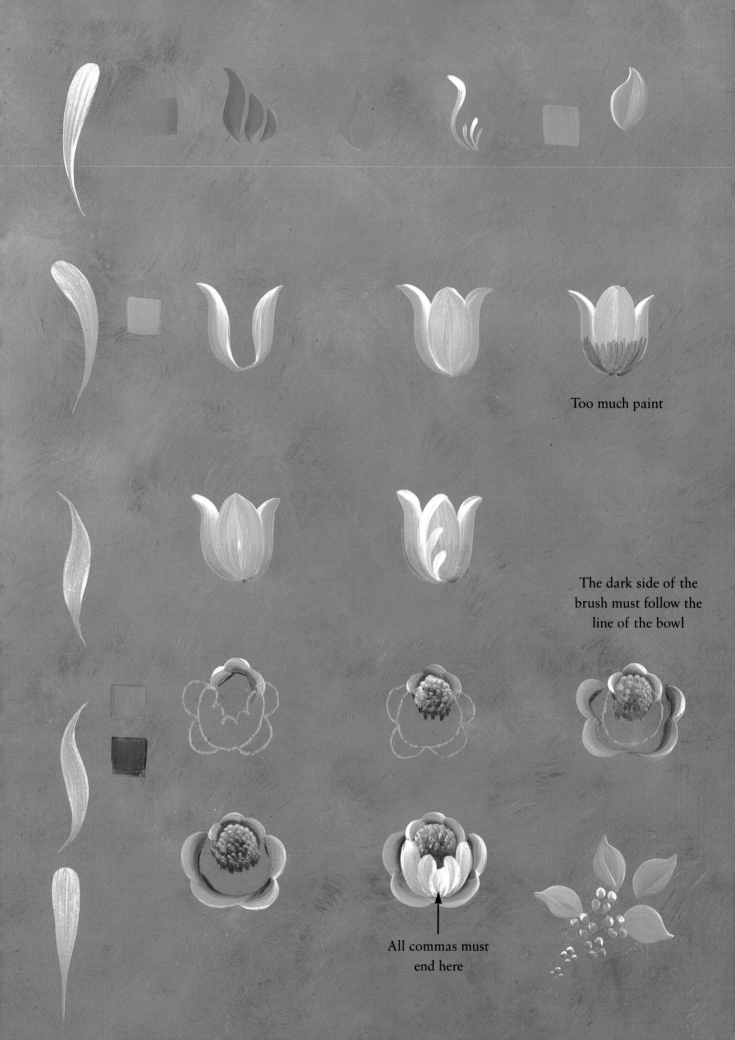

Too much paint

The dark side of the
brush must follow the
line of the bowl

All commas must
end here

with Antique White. The outer petals must
follow the line of the bowl of the rose.
Concentrate on the side of the brush with the
Persian Rose, making sure it follows the line of
the bowl. The other side will take care of itself.
The brush is not flattened for the commas
which make up the bowl of the rose – just use a
round brush loaded with pink and tip loaded
with Antique White.

7 **Tulips** Load the No. 4 brush with Yellow
Oxide lightened with Antique White, tip load
with Antique White and paint the outer petals
with 'S' strokes and the centre petals with
comma strokes. The blush at the base of the
tulip is achieved using a tinting technique (see
page 15). Water down the Persian Rose colour,
resting the brush on a tissue until all the excess
water drains out. Stroke the base of the rose
very lightly, gradually building up the intensity
of colour. If any dots of water appear at the
end of the stroke, the brush is too wet.

8 **Forget-me-nots** Make a marble mix of Plum,
Ultramarine Blue and Antique White. With a
No. 4 brush, pick up varying proportions of
colour so that some flowers are more plum
coloured and others, more pale blue. With this
mix still on the brush, kick load Antique White
on the tip. The forget-me-nots will be
highlighted on one side when you put the brush
down. Make sure that there is enough paint on
the brush so that the tip load of paint touches
the surface, creating perfect, round dots.
Insufficient paint will result in paw prints.

9 **Varnishing** It is essential to be quick with the
first coat of varnish over the crackled area, as
the paint over the crackle glaze may soften and
smudge. Alternatively you could spray varnish
the piece.

Flowers on a wall clock

I used to have a garden bed full of cosmos, borage and pink evening primrose. On this clock I have tried to produce the soft effect of those colours to emulate the appearance of the flowers merging and receding in the summer haze.

MATERIALS

Round brushes No. 2 and 4

Marine sponge with large holes

Varnishing brush

Art carbon

Compass

Damp cloth

Low tack tape

Set square

Stylus

Tracing paper

Water spray

Satin varnish

Colour palette

Olive Green

Antique White

Antique Blue

Antique Green

Leaf Green

Yellow Oxide

Alizarin Crimson

Raw Sienna

Burnt Sienna

Cobalt Blue

INSTRUCTIONS

1 Paint the clock in Olive Green lightened with Antique White.

2 **Marble background** Sponge the surface with a marble mix of 2-parts Antique White to 2-parts Antique Blue and 1-part Antique Green (see page 18 for technique). Wipe the clock with a damp cloth and sponge over the surface, pressing down with a gentle rolling movement of the wrist. Add a little more white to the mix and an extra spray of water and sponge a few loose drifts of this pale colour across the clock until you are satisfied with the effect. Having left it to dry, mix a thin wash of Raw Sienna and very sparingly add a few small drifts with a clean sponge.

3 **Dial and numbers** When the clock is dry, trace the dial and numbers making sure to get them in the right position. Use a set square to draw a straight line down the centre of the clock. This way it's easy to see through the tracing paper whether the twelve and six are vertical. The circles can be painted a number of ways. Block the centre hole of the clock with some tissue. Using the pen extension of an old compass, fill the nib with watered down Antique White paint, and adjust the compass to the required size.

Experiment on paper until you can paint directly and confidently on the clock. Any mistakes can be removed with a damp cloth.

An alternative is to define the circle by freehand with small commas and/or dots. The numbers of the dial are painted using a No. 2 round brush loaded with Antique White.

4   Transfer the design starting with the ribbon, cosmos flowers and leaves. The other motifs should be added after these are painted as many of the small flowers should overlay the leaves.

5   **Ribbon**   Load a No. 4 round brush with an apricot mix of Antique White with a dash of Yellow Oxide and Alizarin Crimson. Side load with Antique White.

6   **Leaves**   With the No. 4 round brush, paint the leaves using the 'S' stroke. Antique Green is used for the larger leaves and a paler shade for the stems and small leaves. To paint the leaf curl, load the brush with Leaf Green and side tip load with Antique White using the wave stroke (see page 23). The decorative comma strokes on the leaves are a pale mix of Antique Green. The small flicked leaves are pale Antique Green, tip loaded with Antique White.

7   **Cosmos flowers**   Each of the flowers is a variation of the apricot colour used for the ribbon. Just add a little more White, Red or Yellow to the mix as you move to each flower so that no two are exactly alike. The paint should be mixed to a watery consistency to give the flowers a translucent look. Paint in the cosmos flowers with the No. 4 brush using the push and pull technique (see page 14). Starting from the centre, tint the base of the petals with a transparent wash of Leaf Green (see page 15). Stipple the stamens with Yellow Oxide and then highlight with a little White over the top of the stamens and Burnt Sienna at the base of the stamens to create shadow. Use the wave stroke to add the petal curl.

8   Trace the rest of the pattern.

9   **Lavender daisies**   Paint the daisies using a No. 2 brush with Antique White and a dash of Cobalt Blue and Alizarin Crimson, tip loaded with Antique White. Vary the flower colour by adding a little more Red or Blue. The centres are stippled with Yellow Oxide.

10   **White bells**   Use a No. 2 round brush loaded with Antique White and paint the white bells using two small comma strokes with flicked up tails. Add three small stamens.

11   **Yellow flowers**   Load the No. 4 round brush with Yellow Oxide kick loaded with Antique White. Keeping the white facing the top of the clock, dot in the petals.

12   **Forget-me-nots**   Load a marble mix of Antique Blue and Antique White on the No. 4 round brush. Dot in the petal and then add the centres with Yellow Oxide.

13   Using a No. 2 brush, add some small decorative commas to the design with Leaf Green, tip loaded with Antique White.

14   **Finishing**   Apply 2-3 coats of satin varnish.

Flip the white to
alternate sides

Push into the white
and pull down

Tint the centre leaf green

Stipple the base

Leave space for the   Stipple the highlight
petal to turn over

Stipple the shadow

12

Cockerel plaque

This cockerel was inspired by an old naïve painting. I wonder if there is such a thing as naïve carpentry? If there is, perhaps my simplistic attempts come into this category! The kitchen tidy is made from left-over, rough-sawn pieces of wood. In keeping with the rustic style, the wood was not sealed.

MATERIALS

Flat brush No. 10

Round brushes
No. 2, 4, 6

Fine marine sponge

Varnishing brush

Art carbon

Low tack tape

Tracing paper

Stylus

Satin varnish

Colour palette

Burnt Sienna

Bold Red

Raw Sienna

Ocean Green

Yellow Oxide

Hooker's Green

Black

INSTRUCTIONS

1 Stain the raw wood with a wash of Raw Sienna.

2 Lightly stipple the front with watery mixes of Raw Sienna, followed by Burnt Sienna with random touches of Hooker's Green.

3 Side load and palette blend the No. 10 flat brush with Burnt Sienna and use this to add a few streaks at ground level for the tufts of dry grass to grow from. Add the tufts with a No. 2 round brush loaded with pale Yellow Oxide.

4 **Border** Load a No. 10 flat shader with a wash of Black to stain the cross bars and edges.

5 **Cockerel** Transfer the cockerel design. With a No. 6 round brush, block in the comb, wattle, front of the neck and chest in Bold Red. The back, tail and wings are Ocean Green and the legs and feet are Black.

6 **Feathers** Load the No. 6 round brush with Ocean Green, tip loaded with Black, and starting at the tip of the tail, paint in the feathers using sweeping strokes. Using the No. 6 round brush, indicate the feathers on the neck, chest and wings with a glaze of translucent Black.

7 **Beak** Load a No. 2 round brush with Yellow Oxide and outline with Black. The nostril is indicated with a Black comma stroke. Add a little shading to the comb by mixing Burnt Sienna with Bold Red. The eye is made up of a large dot of Black with a smaller dot of Yellow Oxide in the centre and an even smaller dot of Black in its centre.

8 **Border** Paint the border using comma strokes with a No. 4 round brush loaded with Yellow Oxide.

9 **Finishing** Apply 2-3 coats of satin varnish to finish. The piece can be hung with a rough string which has been soaked in black tea to discolour it.

Chapter 3

FLAT BRUSH

Flat brush strokes and blending
techniques are used in this chapter
in conjunction with the round
brush work you have covered in the
previous chapter. Here the flat
brush is principally used with side
loading and palette blending
techniques to bring greater depth
and subtle highlights to your work.
Your painting skills will continue to
develop as you learn to incorporate
stroke work using the ruffle
technique and a variety of brush
loading and blending techniques.

Pansy hat box

I was inspired to paint these pansies after a visit to a market where a stallholder had brought the first plants for Spring. After the grey of winter, their vibrant colours seemed quite dazzling. This project focuses on the blending of paint, so it may be appropriate to use the floating technique (see page 15).

MATERIALS

Round brushes No. 2, 4

Flat brushes No. 8, 10

Detail brush 0/10

Marine sponge

Sponge brush

Varnishing brush

Art carbon

Low tack tape

Retarder

Stylus

Tracing paper

Satin varnish

Colour palette

Russian Blue

Indigo

Raw Umber

Antique White

Yellow Oxide

Ocean Green

Hooker's Green

Cadmium Yellow

Persian Rose

Pale Lavender

Burnt Umber

Leaf Green

Burgundy

Purple Dioxide

Burnt Umber
artists' oil paint

INSTRUCTIONS

1 Give the hat box a basecoat of Russian Blue.

2 **Background** Roughly mark the area on the lid and base to be sponged. Create a marble mix of Indigo and Antique White and work this mix with a damp marine sponge. Sponge the lid and base, alternately picking up a little more white or dark blue. Create a wavy edge to divide the plain background from the paint effect. If you use the paints undiluted, the surface will have a slightly textured finish.

3 When the surface is dry, lightly sponge a few drifts of a Raw Umber wash.

4 Transfer the design.

5 **Ribbon** Use the No. 4 round brush loaded with a mid-yellow (Yellow Oxide and Antique White), side loaded with Antique White. Water down the paints so that you get a good sweep. Small holes may appear over the textured surface but this just adds to the distressed effect.

6 **Highlights** Paint the highlight on the ribbon with a No. 8 flat brush. It may be easier to float the paint over a thin layer of water or retarder (see page 10). Side load and palette blend the flat brush with Antique White. With the white side facing the centre of the area to be highlighted, stroke the side loaded brush across the ribbon, then flip the brush over and repeat, butting the white edge to the white edge. Repeat these strokes working away from the centre to create a gradual fading of the highlight. (Alternatively, the dry brush

technique is an effective way of painting highlights – see page 14.)

7 Leaves Load the No. 8 flat brush with Ocean Green and side load on one corner with Yellow Oxide and on the other with Hooker's Green. Blend on the palette and apply the ruffle stroke leaves. Start at the base of the leaf with the brush in the horizontal position. Press down, and zig-zag the brush down one side of the leaf with the Yellow Oxide to the side from which you want the light to come. As you near the tip of the leaf, gradually release the pressure until you are up on the chisel edge. At this point gently roll the brush between your finger and thumb bringing it round to a vertical position on its chisel edge. Then lift off, sweeping the stroke to a point. Flip the brush over and with the Yellow Oxide butting the Hooker's Green, repeat down the other side of the leaf.

8 Add shadow to the base of the leaves that are tucked under the lower petals of the pansy. Float the colour on to the surface (see page 15). Use the No. 8 flat brush, side loaded and blended with Burnt Umber, and float a thin shade of paint on to the base of the leaves (with the dark side of the brush facing the edge of the petals). Use the No. 2 round brush loaded with Hooker's Green and side tip loaded with Leaf Green to add curled edges to the tips of the leaves with the wave stroke (see page 23).

9 Pansies and buds With a No. 4 round brush, paint a basecoat on the first and third pansies and the buds in pale yellow made up from Antique White and Yellow Oxide. The second pansy and its bud should be painted in Pale Lavender. Two or three coats may be needed.

All the petals for the pansies are edged using the ruffle technique. The three different pansies are numbered according to the design template on page 123.

Pansy No. 1 Side load a No. 10 flat brush with Antique White and edge the petals using the ruffle technique (see page 27). Then clean the brush and side load it with a mix of Burgundy and Burnt Umber and use the ruffle technique to shade the centre. With the detail brush, add the little beard in the centre of the flowers in Yellow Oxide.

Pansy No. 2 Side load the No. 10 flat brush with Purple Dioxide and edge the four upper petals using the ruffle technique. The bottom petal should then be edged in Pale Lavender side loaded with Antique White. Side load the brush with Purple Dioxide and shade the centre using the ruffle technique. With the detail brush, add the little beard in the centre of the flowers in Yellow Oxide.

Pansy No. 3 Side load the No. 10 flat brush with Burgundy to which has been added a touch of Burnt Umber. Edge the top petals using the ruffle technique. Then edge the lower three petals with Cadmium Yellow. Overglaze with a narrow band of shading in Persian Rose. Side load the brush with a mix of Burgundy and Burnt Umber and add the centre shading with the ruffle technique. Using a detail brush, add the little beard in the centre in Yellow Oxide.

10 Finishing Erase any remaining pattern lines and lightly antique the surface with Burnt Umber. Leave to dry and varnish after 7-10 days.

Poppy bread bin

When I found this old enamel flour bin, it was looking quite sad with chipped edges. Rather than restore it, I decided to make a feature of its rather worn, rustic look. It was going to be used as a bread bin so I incorporated the golden tones of baked bread with the poppies and cornflowers once so much a part of cornfields.

MATERIALS

Round brushes
No. 2, 4, 6

Flat brush No. 8

2 cm/¾ in. flat brush

5 cm/2 in. sponge brush

Detail brush

Small, fine marine sponge

Soft make-up brush

Varnishing brush

Art carbon

Low tack tape

Stylus

Damp cloth

Retarder

Cocktail stick

Tracing paper

Water spray/atomizer

PVA glue

Antiquing medium

Satin varnish

Colour palette

Antique White

Antique Green

Hooker's Green

Yellow Oxide

Yellow Light

Burnt Sienna

Raw Sienna

Burnt Umber

Alizarin Crimson

Orange Light

Burgundy

Ultramarine Blue

Cobalt Blue

Plum

Burnt Umber artists' oil colour

INSTRUCTIONS

1 **Preparation** When dealing with enamel, make sure that it is cleaned thoroughly (see page 12). Paint the surface with PVA glue mixed with a little water (1-part PVA to 2-3 parts water). Once dry, this will give a good key for the background colour.

2 Using the sponge brush paint a basecoat of Antique White.

3 Wipe the surface of the bread bin with a damp cloth and, while still damp, sponge the surface with a loose marble mix of Raw Sienna and Antique White. Lightly spray with water when working to make the colours blur into each other.

4 Initially, just trace the scroll on to the bread bin.

5 **Scroll** Using the flat brush, block in the scroll with one or two coats of Antique White. If you only use one coat, the shadows of the undercoat create a parchment effect. Use straight, sweeping strokes across the area. Side load and palette blend the 2 cm/¾ in. flat brush with Raw Sienna and add the shading to the inside edges of the scroll. The Raw Sienna should be blended three-quarters of the way

across the brush. If you want more definition, this process can be repeated with Burnt Umber one-quarter of the way across the brush. Use the No. 2 round brush with Burnt Umber to outline the tears in the scroll. Use a mix of the background colour to paint in the tears.

6 When dry, transfer the remaining design.

7 Letters Load a No. 4 round brush with Raw Sienna and tip load with Antique White. Use simple 'S' strokes to form the letters.

8 Leaves With a mix of Hooker's Green and Yellow Oxide loaded on a No. 2 round brush, add the small leaves, flower stems and broken grasses in the background. Paint over the small traced flowers which will be filled in later. With this mix loaded on a No. 4 round brush, paint in the large poppy leaves using comma and 'S' strokes. With the green still on the brush, side tip load with Antique White and edge the poppy leaves with the wave stroke. The same method is used for the cornflower leaves which are painted using Antique Green and Antique White.

9 Corn Paint in the corn using a No. 2 round brush with a marble mix of Burnt Sienna, Raw Sienna and Antique White.

10 Lily-of-the-valley Paint the flowers using a No. 2 round brush loaded with Antique White.

11 Daisies Paint the mauve daisies with a No. 2 brush loaded with Plum and tip loaded with Antique White. The centres are Orange Light stippled with Yellow Light. The white daisies are Antique White with Yellow Light centres.

12 Poppies Paint the poppies using the No. 6 round brush. First load the brush with Orange Light, generously tip loaded with Alizarin Crimson. Drizzle a ragged line with Alizarin Crimson approximately 3-4 stroke widths along the edge of the petal and quickly wipe the excess Alizarin Crimson off the tip of the brush. The brush should still be full of the Orange Light. Using the push/pull technique use comma strokes to fill in the petals. Start the comma just beneath the drizzled line of Alizarin Crimson. Gently push the brush forward into the Alizarin Crimson so that the tip of the brush just catches a little and then pull back with the normal comma stroke. This should leave a ridge of the Alizarin Crimson paint but also pull some of the colour down the petal.

To highlight the petals, dip the brush in retarder and dab off the excess (see page 10). Load with Orange Light and wipe off on a tissue with a stroking motion until there is very little paint left. Stroke the highlight on to the petal, slowly building up the intensity. It is always better to have too little on the brush than too much for dry brush work.

13 Stamens Blot in the centres of the poppies with the No. 4 round brush loaded with Yellow Oxide and tip loaded with Burnt Umber. Use a stylus to add Burnt Umber dots over the centre. Paint the centre of the poppy bud with the No. 4 round brush loaded with Orange Light and tipped with Alizarin Crimson. The calyx is painted the same colour as the poppy leaves. The fine hairs are added with a size 10/0 detail brush.

14 Cornflowers Define the base of the flowers with little dots of Cobalt Blue which are an indication of where to start the clusters of petals which are characteristic of cornflowers. Load a No. 8 flat brush with Ultramarine Blue, side loaded with Antique White. Using the chisel edge of your flat brush, stipple little fans of petals, keeping the Ultramarine Blue to the base of the petal. When you have completed the back row of petals, use a fine marine sponge fixed to a cocktail stick to stipple the centre of the flower (see page 11). Stipple first with a layer of Pale Ultramarine Blue, then Ultramarine Blue and finally, Burgundy. Add the front rows of petals using the same method as the back.

15 Finishing Antique the surface with Burnt Umber and satin varnish after 10 days.

Lion book box

The inspiration for this project which uses an aged, leather look was inspired by heraldic designs, where the tradition of decorative painting was once the preserve of men.

MATERIALS

Round brushes No. 2, 4

0/5 liner brush

2 cm/¾ in. flat brush

5 cm/2 in. sponge brush

5 cm/2 in. coarse household paint brush

Marine sponge

Art carbon

Tracing paper

Low tack tape

Fine sandpaper/000 steel wool

Antiquing medium

Crackle glaze

Satin varnish

Colour palette

Terracotta

Spruce Green

Antique White

Antique Gold

Bold Red

Burnt Umber

Yellow Oxide

Titanium White

Burnt Umber artists' oil colour

INSTRUCTIONS

1 Using a sponge brush, paint the book box with a basecoat of Terracotta inside and out (except the pages, which are Antique White).

2 **Front cover** Apply a coat of crackle glaze to the front cover. When the glaze is dry, sponge over the surface with Spruce Green paint and leave to crackle.

3 **Back cover** Sponge a second thick layer of Terracotta generously on the back and spine of the book. This will create an uneven surface and help to give the impression of leather. When this is dry, paint over in Spruce Green using the sponge brush. When this coat has dried, take some fine sandpaper or 000 steel wool and rub over the green until the spots of the Terracotta start to show through.

4 **Pages** Paint the leaves of the book around the edge of the box in Antique White using the 2 cm/¾ in. flat brush. Make up a mix of 4-parts satin varnish to 1-part Antique Gold with a dash of Burnt Umber. Working one side at a time, apply this mix and quickly drag your coarse household brush across the surface, creating an impression of book leaves (see the step-by-step photographs on page 96).

5 Trace the outline of the lion on the front cover.

6 **Lion** Block in the lion with Yellow Oxide loaded on a No. 4 round brush (it may need 2-3 coats). Then give it a top coat of Antique Gold. When dry, trace the detail of the face and fur on to the lion's body. Paint the eye Titanium White with a No. 2 round brush and dot the centre with Burnt Umber. Paint the tongue and claws in Bold Red. Load the No. 2 round brush with Burnt Umber and outline the lion and tufts of fur. Mask off the centre panel of the front cover and frame it with gold paint.

7 **Finishing** Erase all chalk lines and antique with Burnt Umber.

Scroll wastebin

The Arts and Crafts Museum in Moscow exhibits a range of beautifully decorated late eighteenth- and early nineteenth-century Russian distaffs. The scrolls on this bin were influenced by one of these pieces. When spinning, the distaff prevents the wool or flax from touching the floor. The bin is made of papier mâché, which I really enjoy working with because its surface has a subtle texture that enhances the decoration.

MATERIALS

Round brush No. 1 or 0/5 liner

Round brush No. 6

5 cm/2 in. sponge brush

Varnishing brush

Art carbon

Tracing paper

Stylus

Tack cloth

000 fine steel wool

Varnish

Colour palette

Parisian Yellow

Terracotta

Indigo

Olive Green

Burnt Umber artists' oil paint

INSTRUCTIONS

The position of the colours is indicated on the design template (see page 126) by their first letter. If you dot the colours on to the tracing, it will act as a quick reference while painting.

1 Using a 5 cm/2 in. sponge brush, paint a basecoat of Parisian Yellow on the exterior of the bin and Terracotta on the interior.

2 Transfer the pattern.

3 With the No. 6 round brush, block in the colours, following the shapes with your strokes.

4 **Lines** Using a No. 1 round brush or the liner brush, outline the blocks of colour in Indigo and add the fine commas and scrolls.

5 When this is dry, erase any carbon marks and distress the bin by rubbing it down with 000 fine steel wool. This will cut back the paint and weaken the intensity of the colours. Wipe clean with a tack cloth and antique the piece with Burnt Umber (see page 16).

6 Leave to dry for a few days before varnishing.

Tip It is not necessary to wash the sponge brushes out between coats of paint – just wrap them tightly in plastic and squeeze out all the air.

Blackberry breadboard

The idea for painting this breadboard came to me whilst visiting Russia. I was fortunate enough to visit several typical country homes in which I saw decorated wooden items in everyday use – including bread and cheeseboards. For this project, only one side needs decoration as the other side is used to cut the bread. I created a wood stain effect by thinning the paint with water, thus allowing the grain of the wood to show through the design.

MATERIALS	Colour palette
Round brush No. 2	Yellow Oxide
Detail brush 10/0	Antique White
Flat brushes No. 4, 6	Hooker's Green
Varnishing brush	Burgundy
Art carbon (red)	Terracotta
Stylus	Persian Rose
Tracing paper	Burnt Sienna
Low tack tape	
Retarder	
Satin varnish/sealer	

INSTRUCTIONS

1 Seal the wood with 2 thin coats of satin varnish or sealer.

2 **Transfer the design** A red carbon and very light pressure should be used as some of the carbon lines may be seen through the thin glaze of the paint.

3 Load a No. 2 round brush with Yellow Oxide and side tip load with Burnt Sienna, and paint in the stems (keeping the Burnt Sienna to the underside of the stems). With a detail brush, add the thorns using comma strokes.

4 **Leaves** Load the No. 6 flat brush with retarder and remove excess by resting the brush on a tissue until the sheen disappears. Load the brush with Hooker's Green one side and Yellow Oxide on the other and blend this well on the palette. The Yellow Oxide should blend right into the green to turn it a lighter shade. Paint in all the leaves using the ruffle stroke (see page 27).

The veins of the leaves are added with the detail brush using a mix of Yellow Oxide and Hooker's Green. Side load the No. 6 flat brush with Persian Rose, blend to a fine glaze on the palette and randomly add a blush to some of the leaves.

5 **Blackberries** The berries towards the base of the stem are darker than those at the tip. With the No. 6 flat brush, basecoat the darker berries in a pale mix of Burgundy and Antique White. Wash the brush and side load with Burgundy, then define the cells with small 'C' strokes. Add emphasis to some of the cells by adding a little Purple Dioxide to the Burgundy. When dry, go over the whole berry with a wash of this mix.

6 Light berries These do not need a base colour if you are working on a light background. However, on a dark surface, the berries should be given a pale basecoat. Side load the brush with a pale mix of Burgundy and Antique White and use 'C' strokes to define the cells on one side. Repeat this process on the other side using the brush side loaded with a pale lime green (Hooker's Green and Yellow Oxide). Overstroke the pink cells with Burgundy using tiny 'C' strokes, adding all the cells on the red side of the berry. Gradually work towards the centre, allowing the intensity of colour to fade away. Overstroke the cells on the green side of the berry with the brush side loaded with Antique White.

7 Add shine to the cells of all the berries by side loading the corner of the brush with a small amount of Antique White. Decide from which direction the light is to come and highlight individual cells on that side of the berry. Accentuate the highlight with the 10/0 detail brush by adding commas in Antique White on the contours of some cells.

8 Blossom Paint the petals with ruffled 'C' strokes using the No. 4 flat brush, side loaded with Antique White. Clean the brush and side load with a wash of Persian Rose to add a blush at the base of the petals. The centres are stippled in a pale mix of Yellow Oxide and Antique White and the tips of the stamens are fine dots of Antique White applied with a stylus.

9 Finishing Erase any carbon marks and apply 2-3 coats of satin varnish.

Naïve clock

The idea for the pattern on this clock came from a wall panel painted by William Price in 1831 displayed in the Francis du Pont Winterthur Museum, USA. In the second quarter of the nineteenth century, there was a fashion for murals painted in shades of brown and green. I find the use of such a limited palette very appealing, where naïve motifs and a simple use of colour are combined with a carefully structured design.

MATERIALS

Flat brushes
No. 8, 10, 18

Round brushes
No. 1, 2, 4

Deer foot stippler No. 6

5 cm/2 in. sponge brush

Fine marine sponge

Varnishing brush

Art carbon (yellow)

Tracing paper

Stylus

Liquid masking

Low tack tape

Crackle glaze

Retarder

Satin varnish

Colour palette

Antique White

Antique Blue

Antique Green

Terracotta

Olive Green

Hooker's Green

Burnt Umber

Burnt Sienna

Raw Sienna

Payne's Grey

INSTRUCTIONS

1 Give the clock a basecoat of Antique White mixed with a touch of Olive Green.

2 Apply the crackle glaze to the whole of the clock and leave to dry.

3 Apply a wash of very pale Antique Blue over the crackle glaze, using a 5 cm/2 in. sponge brush (this is better than an ordinary brush as it holds more paint and makes it easier to travel across the surface before running out of paint). Use strokes that sweep from side to side across the clock. This uneven wash begins the effect of the sky and water.

4 Trace the pattern with yellow carbon which will not show through the washes. With a dark carbon, the lines will show through the washes and once under the paint, will not rub off.

5 **Water effect** Create a water effect for the lake using a No. 8 flat brush, side loaded with a thin wash of Antique Green. Use random strokes across the lake with the colour on the side pointing to the top of the clock. Repeat with Raw Sienna and Payne's Grey.

6 **Hills** Using a No. 18 flat brush loaded with a wash of Payne's Grey, Raw Sienna and Hooker's Green, paint the hills in the background with the strokes following the shape of the hills. When dry, go over them with a wash of Antique Green and Raw Sienna. Emphasize the outline of the hills by shading them using the same brush side loaded with a wash of Payne's Grey.

7 Fields Before painting in the background colours of the fields, apply liquid masking to the tree trunk to avoid building up too much depth of colour (see page 10). Finely stipple the fields outside the house using a fine marine sponge. Apply the paint in three layers, allowing the paint to dry in between each layer. Start with Raw Sienna. Then finely stipple with Hooker's Green and finally lightly stipple with Burnt Sienna. The field in the foreground was done in the same way but using more Burnt Sienna to make it darker. Using a No. 10 flat brush side loaded with a mix of Burnt Sienna and Burnt Umber, define the edge of the field in the background where it meets the water's edge. In the same way differentiate the foreground field from the background field and lake.

8 House Using a No. 18 flat brush loaded with Antique White, block in the walls. For the roof, use Payne's Grey.

9 Windows Side load and palette blend a No. 6 flat brush with Burnt Umber. The windows are indicated by shadows. Keeping the side load to the right side of the windows, stroke in the shadows so that they disappear on the left. The door is painted using Burnt Umber loaded all the way across the brush. Add the dormer window using a No. 1 round brush loaded with Burnt Umber.

10 Grass Mix Hooker's Green and Burnt Sienna on the No. 2 round brush and stroke in the tufts of grass.

11 Tree Peel off the masking and paint the bark of the tree. With a No. 4 round brush, stroke random washes of Burnt Sienna, Payne's Grey and Raw Sienna down the trunk and along the branches. If necessary use a No. 2 round brush for the finer branches.

12 Bushes and leaves To create the fine effect of leaves on the tree, water down a mix of Hooker's Green, Raw Sienna and Burnt Umber. Dip a No. 6 deer foot stippler into the paint, dab off the excess until almost dry and stipple the leaves. Use Antique Green for the bushes and accentuate with Hooker's Green.

13 Lady Paint the lady with a No. 1 round brush. The skin tones consist of a very pale mix of Terracotta and Antique White. The hair and shawl are painted in Burnt Sienna. The dress is a mix of Hooker's Green and Burnt Sienna. The frills on the dress are Burnt Umber. The angler, the man in the boat and the boat are all painted in Burnt Sienna.

14 Fence Paint using a No. 1 round brush loaded with Burnt Sienna.

15 The hours on the naïve clock can be indicated by small dots or triangles.

16 Finishing Lightly antique and then varnish.

Nautical lap desk

This ship was inspired by an old painting my husband had in his antique shop. You could adapt a picture of any ship into a design such as this. It really isn't difficult and I have broken it down into easy-to-follow steps.

MATERIALS

Round brushes No. 1, 2, 3, 4

Flat brushes No. 6, 8, 10 and 2 cm/¾ in.

5/0 liner brush

1.3 cm/½ in. comb brush

5 cm/2 in. sponge brush

Varnishing brush

Art carbon

Tracing paper

Low tack tape

Stylus

Fine sandpaper/000 steel wool

Antiquing medium

Crackle glaze

Matt or satin varnish

Colour palette

Russian Blue

Antique White

Yellow Oxide

Raw Sienna

Cerulean Blue

Burnt Umber

Ocean Green

Antique Gold

Indigo

Alizarin Crimson

Terracotta

Hooker's Green

Payne's Grey

Burnt Sienna

Burnt Umber artists' oil colour

INSTRUCTIONS

1 **Basecoat** Apply 2-3 coats of Russian Blue to the exterior and Terracotta to the interior using the sponge brush. The edges of the lid and base are painted Terracotta with Antique Gold applied roughly using your finger.

2 Only trace the outline of the centre panel and the flags which decorate the top and edges of the desk.

3 **Centre panel** Block in the centre panel with Antique White, using a No. 10 flat brush. Don't worry if it is not perfectly white as this will heighten its distressed appearance.

4 **Crackle glaze** Apply the crackle glaze using the 5 cm/2 in. sponge brush or a No. 8 flat brush to the centre panel, and the flags and scrolls decorating the lid and sides. Leave to dry (see page 17). When dry, apply a coat of Antique White which will then crackle. This can be applied either with a brush or a sponge. Remember not overstroke the crackle while it is wet as it will disturb the crazing.

5 **Flags and scrolls** With the No. 8 flat brush, paint the flags and scrolls decorating the lid and sides (see worksheet on page 85).

6 **Sky** Mark the horizon. Side load the 2 cm/¾ in. flat brush with a pale, sky blue wash of Cerulean Blue and Antique White. Starting at the top of the panel, with the blue side load pointing to the top, work your way down the panel. Sweep from side to side, allowing the paint to fade to almost nothing a third of the way down the sky. Side load the brush with a wash of Yellow Oxide and repeat

this technique, starting with the colour next to the horizon and working your way up to meet the pale blue of the sky.

7 Clouds Add a few random sweeps of an Ocean Green wash across the top half of the sky. Disturb the paint by rubbing it with your finger, using a circular motion. Repeat with Indigo, bringing the colour in from the corners. Add a little Antique White to the edge of the clouds, using your finger.

8 Sea Paint with a wash of Ocean Green using a 2 cm/¾ in. flat brush. Load the No. 10 flat brush with Hooker's Green and add the waves with a chopping action. Create shade beneath the ship by adding some Indigo. With a No. 5/0 liner brush, drizzle a little white across the top of some waves. Use a 2 cm/¾ in. comb brush to pull the white paint down the waves with a curving motion.

9 Trace the pattern of the ship and sails but do not trace any of the ropes or ladders yet.

10 Sails Using a 2 cm/¾ in. flat brush, block in the sails with Antique White (see page 14). Use a 5/0 liner brush loaded with Yellow Oxide to paint the seams on the sails. The telltales (ribbons sewn to the sail to indicate wind direction) are painted in Raw Sienna with a tiny dot of Indigo at the top. Side load and palette blend a 2 cm/¾ in. flat brush with a wash of Burnt Umber to shade the sails as indicated on the worksheet.

11 Ship Using a No. 2 round brush, paint the line on the side of the ship in Alizarin Crimson. Use a No. 6 flat brush loaded with Indigo to paint the main body of the ship.

12 Trace the rigging and all remaining details.

13 Masts and rigging Load a No. 1 round brush with Burnt Sienna, side tip loaded with Burnt Umber on one side and Yellow Oxide on the other. Paint in the masts, keeping the Burnt Umber to the left. The spars and the small people are painted with Burnt Umber. The cabin is Raw Sienna with a Burnt Sienna roof. The lifeboat is painted in Antique White. Using a No. 5/0 liner brush loaded with Indigo, add all the ropes and ladders, and outline the sails.

14 Flags on the ship Paint the background of the flags with Antique White, using a No. 1 round brush and then add decorative details (see worksheet on page 85).

15 The ships in the distance are indicated using a No. 6 flat brush loaded with a very pale mix of Payne's Grey and Antique White.

16 Frame The picture is framed using comma strokes painted with a No. 4 round brush, loaded with Terracotta and tip loaded with Antique Gold.

17 Finishing When completely dry, use very fine sandpaper (or 000 steel wool) over the desk to distress the edges and corners (which are most likely to have suffered the wear and tear of time). Erase any remaining traced lines, dust off and antique the lap desk with Burnt Umber. Leave for a few days before varnishing.

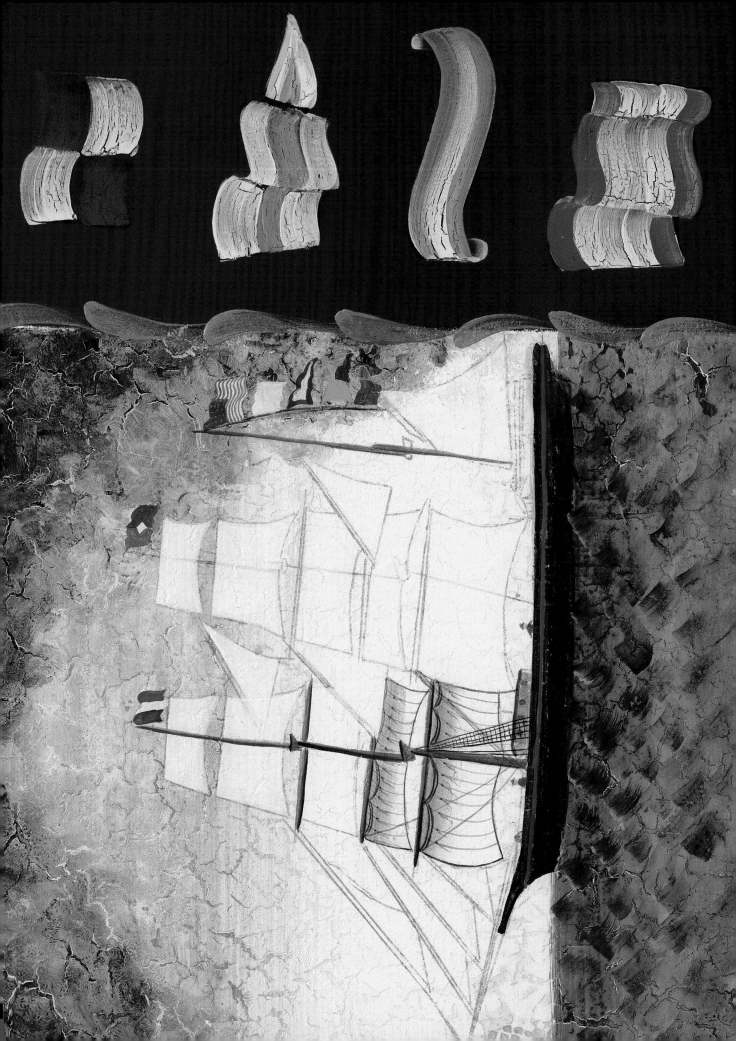

Chapter 4
CLASSIC PAINTING

The projects in this chapter bring
together a range of classic styles
influenced by Russian, early
American and French furniture,
and objets d'art. The designs use
all the different round and flat
brush techniques which you have
learnt in the previous chapters.

Rose and tulip tray

The design for the spray of flowers on this tray was influenced by the beautiful collection of eighteenth-century Sèvres porcelain which can be seen at the Wallace Collection in London. This small museum is a great source of inspiration and well worth a visit.

MATERIALS

Round brushes
No. 1, 2, 3

Flat brush No. 8

Detail brush 10/0

No. 4 deer foot stippler

5 cm/2 in. sponge brush

Marine sponge

Varnishing brush

Art carbon

Tracing paper

Stylus

Low tack tape

Retarder

Satin/gloss varnish

Colour palette

Russian Blue

Turquoise

Ocean Green

Cobalt Blue

Antique Gold

Hooker's Green

Yellow Oxide

Antique White

Burgundy

Purple Dioxide

Persian Rose

Terracotta

Burnt Umber

Ultramarine Blue

Yellow Light

Cadmium Yellow

INSTRUCTIONS

1 **Basecoat** Paint the entire tray with Russian Blue, using a 5 cm/2 in. sponge brush. When dry, make a loose marble mix of 2-parts Ocean Green to 1-part Cobalt Blue and 1-part Turquoise. Sponging into corners can be awkward so mask off the base and sides alternately. A deer foot stippler is used to stipple in the angle between the rim and the base. When dry, use your finger to rub Antique Gold along the edge and inside the handles.

2 Transfer the pattern.

3 **Rose leaves** Load the No. 3 round brush with a mid-green (Hooker's Green, Yellow Oxide and Antique White), and block in the leaves. Using the same green, side tip load with Antique White and follow the outer edges of the leaves with the wave stroke. Wipe off and flatten the brush on a tissue. With the semi-dry brush, pull the Antique White from the edges of the leaves down towards the centre. Tint the base and centre of the leaves with a wash of Hooker's Green. Use a No. 5/0 fine liner with the same wash to paint the veins.

4 **Tulip leaves** Load the No. 3 round brush with the mix of mid-green, side tip loaded with Hooker's Green on one side and Antique White on the other. Use flowing 'S' strokes.

5 **Small leaves** These are made up of little fat 'S' strokes using a No. 2 round brush, loaded with a very pale mix of green and side tip loaded with Antique White.

6 **Stems** Paint the stems with the No. 1 round brush loaded with a pale green watered down to an inky consistency.

7 Roses Basecoat each rose using a No. 3 round brush. The roses are different shades of pale Terracotta and pale Burgundy. When dry, use a No. 8 flat brush, side loaded in a deeper shade of their initial colour to shade the centre and base of each rose using a 'C' stroke. With a thin wash of Cadmium Yellow, tint the inside of the bowl of the roses. Working one rose at a time, apply a thin layer of retarder (see page 10). Load the No. 3 round brush with water and side tip load with Antique White. Starting with the back petals use 'C' strokes and the wave stroke to put in all the petals on the bowl of the rose. The outer petals are painted from the base upwards. Turn one or two petals over using the wave stroke.

8 Blue flowers Load the No. 3 round brush with Antique White, tip loaded with Ultramarine Blue. Paint in the back petals using the push/pull technique. Stipple the centre with Yellow Oxide, tip loaded with Antique White, and then add the front petals.

9 Yellow flowers Load the No. 2 round brush with Yellow Oxide, side loaded with Antique White. Each petal is made up from two facing comma strokes (with the side load of Antique White on the outside edges).

10 White flowers Finely stipple the centre of the flowers with a mid-green wash, using a marine sponge on a cocktail stick. Paint the petals with small comma strokes, using a No. 2 round brush loaded with Antique White. Stipple the centres with Yellow Light.

11 Tulips Load the No. 3 round brush with Antique White and block in both tulips. For the Burgundy tulip, reload with Antique White and side tip load with Burgundy. Use the wave stroke to outline the petal, wipe off excess on a tissue and pull a little colour in from the edges. Do not take the colour all the way to the base of the petal. When dry, make a very pale yellow mix of Yellow Light and Antique White. Turn the tulip upside-down, and tint the base by pulling the wash down from the base. Use the same method for the Persian Rose tulip but paint the base with Antique White. If the brush leaves a little puddle of paint when tinting, it is too wet. Simply rest the bristles on a tissue and start again. Stipple a little Yellow Oxide at the base of the stamens and paint in three stamens using Burnt Umber. Add the bases and stem using a No. 1 round brush loaded with pale green and side loaded with Hooker's Green.

12 Michelmas daisies Use a No. 1 round brush loaded with Purple Dioxide, wiped through a little Antique White. Paint the back row using little comma strokes. These petals must reach past the start of the stamens, so that they are tucked in behind them. Follow this by stippling the stamens of the flowers with the same brush loaded with Yellow Oxide and tip loaded with Antique White. Add the front rows of petals. The design template indicates single rows of petals, but add more as shown opposite on the worksheet.

13 Finishing Apply 2-3 coats of satin or gloss varnish.

Fruit basket on cabinet

This cabinet is painted in a monochrome, French Provincial style. The majority of the design is applied using a glaze of Indigo, side loaded and palette blended on to the flat brushes. Practise different elements of the pattern until you feel confident. This will also help you decide just how dark or light you would like the colour.

MATERIALS

Flat brushes
No. 6, 10, 18

Round brushes No. 2, 4

5 cm/2 in. sponge brush

Liner brush

Art carbon (blue)

Tracing paper

Low tack tape

Stylus

000 fine steel wool

Cling film

Cotton buds

Old toothbrush

Retarder

Antiquing medium

Satin varnish

Gloss varnish

Colour palette

Antique White

Indigo

Payne's Grey

Payne's Grey artists'
oil colour

INSTRUCTIONS

1 **Basecoat** Give the cabinet 2-3 coats of Antique White.

2 Transfer the fruit pattern on to the cabinet. This project uses thin washes of paint so a blue or water soluble art carbon should be used as the carbon lines may show beneath the glaze.

3 **Glaze** Mix some satin varnish or clear glazing medium with 2-3 drops retarder in a small dish. This medium will always be loaded on the brush before the Indigo is side loaded and blended. Because the mix has more body than water, it gives more control when using this technique on larger areas. Do not use white to reduce the shade as this will change the whole effect. Care must be taken not to overlap lines as all mistakes will show through the glaze. A damp cotton bud used quickly will mop up any overlaps. You may find it easier to use liquid masking to prevent the different elements from overlapping each other.

4 **Fruit leaves** These are painted using the ruffle technique. Both flat brushes are side loaded and palette blended with the Indigo glaze. Use the No. 18 flat brush for the grape leaves and the No. 6 flat brush for the apple leaves.

5 **Fruit** The No. 18 flat brush is used for the large pieces of fruit and the No. 10 flat brush is used for the grapes. With the brushes side loaded as required, use smooth sweeping strokes to outline the fruit with a soft blending of colour (see worksheet on page 94).

6 Stems Paint the stems with the No. 2 round brush loaded with the glaze mix and side tip loaded with Indigo.

7 Basket The coiled straw effect on the rim and base of the basket is made from a series of 'S' strokes using a No. 6 flat brush, side loaded with the Indigo glaze. Apply the criss-cross lines of the basket weave by keeping the dark edge of the side loaded brush pointing to the base of the basket. When dry, side load the No. 18 flat brush and shade the sides of the basket, as well as below the rim and base.

8 Butterfly and birds Side load the No. 6 flat brush and paint in the birds. Use the ruffle technique for the butterfly wings.

9 Leaves Load the No. 4 round brush with the Indigo glaze and paint the small sprays of leaves and those around the door using simple 'S' strokes.

10 Panels Side load the No. 18 flat brush with Indigo and paint the shading for the faux panels on the sides and door of the cabinet. To apply the straight lines on the side panel when there are no mouldings to follow, cut a 3 x 3 cm (1½ x 1½ in.) piece of straight timber to the length needed for your panels. Attach thick sticky felt pads on one side. This will hold it just above the surface to be painted, making it an excellent straight edge against which to rest the brush. If you have a steady hand, low tack tape is an alternative method.

11 Lightly fly speck the front and sides of the cabinet with a wash of Indigo (see page 15). Once this is dry, the lower part of the cabinet is ready to be distressed and antiqued. Rub the painting back with 000 fine steel wool and antique with Payne's Grey (see page 16).

12 Marble top The marbled effect on the top of the cabinet is created with a glaze of Payne's Grey and satin varnish with a few drops of retarder. Slosh this (yes, really!) over the surface, quickly lay a sheet of cling film and lift off straight away. This will leave a marbled effect. Study the design left by the cling film and use a damp cloth to lift out a few patches of the colour. Leave to dry. Add a little more Payne's Grey to the glaze and emphasize some of the lines using a liner brush (or goose feather), especially around the patches which have had the colour taken out.

13 Finishing When this is dry, apply several coats of gloss varnish.

Tip Low tack tape can be used to mitre the corners when running the shading down the edge of the panels.

Lace book box

The design on this book box was inspired as much by pictures of antique gold and silver filigree caskets as by antique pieces of lace which belonged to my mother. I find it fascinating to see how designs and artefacts reflect the period in which they were made. Although this design looks intricate, it consists mainly of comma strokes and just requires a little patience!

MATERIALS	Colour palette
Round brush No. 2	*Terracotta*
Flat brush No. 4	*Black*
2 cm/¾ in. flat brush	*Antique White*
Liner No. 5/0	*Antique Gold*
Coarse household brush	*Burnt Umber*
30 cm/12 in. sponge brush	*Burnt Umber artists' oil paint*
Soft make-up brush	
Stylus	
Tracing paper	
Art carbon	
Low tack tape	
Antiquing medium	
Satin varnish	

INSTRUCTIONS

1 **Basecoat** With a sponge brush paint the outside of the book box Black (the page leaves are Antique White) and the interior Terracotta.

2 **Pages** Paint the leaves of the book around the edge of the box in Antique White using the 2 cm/¾ in. flat brush. Then make up a mix of 4-parts satin varnish to 1-part Antique Gold with a dash of Burnt Umber. Working one side at a time, apply this mix and then quickly drag your coarse household brush across the surface, creating the impression of book leaves.

3 Trace the design The design template which is a quarter section needs to be traced on each corner of the book box.

4 Lines Start by painting the lines with the 5/0 liner. Try to paint them all at the same sitting as you will build up a rhythm with the spacing.

5 Roses To paint in the roses use a No. 4 flat brush loaded with clear glazing medium or satin varnish, side loaded with Antique White. Use small commas for the petals and the wave stroke for the bowl of the rose.

6 Decide which of the motifs you will paint next and apply them with the No. 2 round brush. I find it useful to paint all the same elements in the design together and then move on to the next set.

7 Dots All the dots are applied with the stylus. The graduated dots on the border are created by dipping your stylus into a pool of paint. Start at the top of the peak and without reloading, travel down the line (the dots will decrease in size as the paint runs out). If you need the dots to be uniform in size, renew the paint on the stylus every two dots.

8 Finishing Once dry, this can be antiqued with Burnt Umber or just varnished.

Roses and ribbon chair

The inspiration for this design was drawn from the decorative furniture painting of the Regency period. I found this small chair in a market and cleaned it up using a steel wool soap pad which is a trick used by antique dealers for removing heat marks on old furniture without scratching the surface. Thoroughly wet the pad before use and make sure to wash all the soap off the surface when you have finished. I used a very fine grade sandpaper on the design area to give a key for the acrylic paint. Any fine scratch marks from the sanding disappear beneath a coat of varnish.

MATERIALS

Round brush No. 3

Flat brush No. 6

Liner brush No. 1

Varnishing brush

Tracing paper

Art carbon

Stylus

Low tack tape

Oil-based satin or gloss varnish

Colour palette

Alizarin Crimson

Yellow Oxide

Antique White

Turquoise

Hooker's Green

Yellow Light

Burnt Umber

INSTRUCTIONS

1 Trace the pattern.

2 **Ribbon** Load a pale mix of turquoise, side loaded with Antique White on a No. 3 round brush. Use 'S' strokes, alternating the White from side to side to create a rippled ribbon.

3 **Leaves** Make up a mix of pale green using the Hooker's Green and Yellow Oxide. Load the No. 3 round brush and using simple 'S' strokes block in all the large leaves. Side load the No. 6 flat brush with Yellow Light and blend to a fine wash. Decide which way the light is coming from and highlight that side of the leaves with Yellow Light. Repeat this on the opposite side with a fine wash of Burnt Umber.

4 With the Hooker's Green loaded on the No. 3 round brush, side tip loaded with Yellow Oxide, paint in the stem and centre vein keeping the Yellow Oxide to the side of the light source. With the No. 6 flat brush side loaded with a wash of Burnt Umber, add a little shade behind the centre vein. Mix a thin wash of Antique White, load the No. 1 liner brush and outline the leaf and add the fine veins. Load the No. 3 brush with this wash, wipe off until almost dry and add a little extra highlight on the top of the leaf (see page 14).

5 **Small leaves** The small filler leaves are painted with simple 'S' strokes. Use the No. 3 round brush loaded with a mid-green made up from Hooker's Green and Yellow Oxide, mixed to a thin glaze with satin varnish or a glazing medium.

6 Roses Mix a deep rose pink using Alizarine Crimson, Yellow Oxide and Antique White and a paler rose pink by adding more of the Antique White. Basecoat the roses in the pale rose pink with the No. 3 round brush. Side load the brush with the deep rose pink to shade the centre and base of the bowl. Load the brush with the pale rose pink, flatten and side load with Antique White and paint the petals at the back of the rose using comma strokes.

7 Stamens Now add the stamens using the No. 6 flat brush loaded with the dark rose pink and side loaded with Yellow Oxide. Stipple the stamens using the chisel end of the brush with the Yellow Oxide pointing towards the top of the rose. With the No. 3 round brush, add the rest of the petals using comma and wave strokes with the pale rose pink side loaded with Antique White.

8 Yellow flowers Load the No. 3 round brush with a pale mix of Yellow Oxide and tip loaded with Antique White. The petals are painted using fat little comma strokes. The centres are pale green stippled with a circle of Persian Rose mixed with Yellow Oxide.

9 When dry, finish off with an oil-based varnish.

Spring flower mirror

This mirror was inspired by a beautiful old tray that was brought in to class by one of my students. We were all captivated by the wonderful feeling of Spring that these wild flowers evoked. I hope you enjoy painting it as much as I did. The design lends itself well to enlargement. The amount of detail used in the centres of the flowers depends on how much the pattern is scaled up or down. There are instructions for painting small and large strawberries if you should wish to use elements of this pattern in other ways.

MATERIALS

Round brushes No. 1, 2

Detail brush No. 0/5

2 marine sponges, one with fine and one with large holes

5 cm/2 in. sponge brush

Varnishing brush

Art carbon

Tracing paper

Stylus

Low tack tape

Satin varnish

Colour palette

Yellow Light

Antique White

Plum

Lavender

Black

Hooker's Green

Yellow Oxide

Ultramarine Blue

Bright Green

Burgundy

Bold Red

Alizarin Crimson

Cadmium Yellow

Burnt Sienna

Raw Umber

INSTRUCTIONS

1 **Basecoat** Give the mirror a basecoat of Black using the 5 cm/2 in. sponge brush. When this is dry, make a wash of olive green by mixing Black and Yellow Oxide. With a damp marine sponge (with large holes), lightly stipple the frame, allowing the Black to show through.

2 Transfer the pattern.

3 **Leaves** Paint in all the leaves and flower stems using a No. 2 round brush. The daffodil stems and leaves are a mix of Hooker's Green and Yellow Light. The remaining leaves are Hooker's Green and Yellow Oxide. Block in the strawberry leaves with a mid-green, made up from Hooker's Green and Yellow Oxide. When this is dry, paint in the small commas on one side of the leaves using a paler mix of the base colour. On the other side of the leaves, make the commas a shade darker than the base colour.

4 **Small strawberries** Block the berries in with Yellow Oxide on a No. 2 round brush. When this is dry, paint over them with Bold Red. Tint one side of the berry Alizarin Crimson and the other side Yellow Oxide. Paint the seeds in Yellow Oxide with the detail brush.

5 **Large strawberries** Block in the berries with Yellow Oxide, and paint over a coat of Bold

Red using a No. 4 round brush. With a No. 8 flat brush side loaded and blended with Alizarin Crimson, add a darker shade on one side of the berry. Stipple the highlight with a fine marine sponge dipped in Yellow Light. Paint in the seeds using a No. 1 round brush loaded with Burnt Sienna. Repeat by going over the Burnt Sienna seeds with smaller Yellow Oxide strokes (see page 105).

6 **White flowers** Paint in the strawberry flowers with a No. 2 round brush, loaded with Antique White and flattened and side loaded with more Antique White. Each petal is made up of two small comma strokes facing each other, with the extra side load of Antique White to the outer edges. Stipple the centres with pale Yellow Oxide.

7 **Burgundy flowers** Load the No. 2 round brush with Antique White side loaded with Burgundy. The petals are a pair of pointed commas with the side loaded Burgundy facing the middle of the petal. The centre is a circle of Yellow Light dots.

8 **Forget-me-nots** Load and tip load a No. 2 round brush with a marble mix of Ultramarine Blue, Plum, and Antique White. Dot in the petals, constantly tip loading with the various colours in the marble mix. This will create an interesting variation of colour in the petals. Dot the centres with Antique White. When dry, add a small black dot in the centre of the white dot. Toothpicks and the end of the brush handle dipped in paint are also effective ways of making dots for small flowers. Forget-me-nots are often referred to as filler flowers. They should also be known as the 'rescue service', as many a forget-me-not has hidden a mistake!

9 **Bluebells** Blend a mixture of Plum and Ultramarine Blue with a little Antique White on a No. 2 round brush. The bluebell buds have a mauve tinge. The mix should have more Plum when you start at the top of the stem, with the flowers turning blue as you go down the stem. The bells are little comma strokes with flicked up ends. Give the bells a basecoat of Ultramarine Blue if they are being painted on a dark background.

10 **Daisies** Load the No. 2 round brush with Antique White, tipped very lightly in Bold Red. Stroke the brush out on the palette, and then tip load again in Antique White, so that there is just a hint of the red in the comma strokes for the petals. Make sure that the ends of the strokes all point to the centre of the base of the flower. This means that if the stroke was continued, it would arrive at the centre of the flower. It is very important to note that when painting any flower, the petals need to point to the centre of the growth; otherwise they will look square. The centres are stippled in pale Yellow Light and highlighted with tiny dots of Antique White.

11 **Clovers** Paint these flowers with the No. 2 round brush using little comma strokes, once again using shades of Plum and Burgundy.

12 **Narcissus** Paint the back petals with a No. 2 round brush loaded with a mix of Cadmium Yellow, Antique White and Yellow Oxide and side tip loaded with Antique White. Use two strokes as shown on the worksheet, keeping the White on the outer edge of the petals. Stipple the centre of the trumpet with a mix of Yellow Light, Bright Green and Antique White to make a pale lime green. Load the

No. 2 round brush with the mix for the petal and tip load this with Bold Red. Drizzle a very fine line of Bold Red along the edge of the trumpet, wipe the excess off the brush and use the push/pull technique to pull the paint down to the centres. Then add the rest of the petals.

13 Primrose Use the No. 2 round brush with the same yellow mix as the narcissus, with a little more Yellow Oxide added. With a No. 1 round brush or a stylus, dot the centre of the primroses in a mix of Hooker's Green and Yellow Oxide followed by Bright Green mixed with Yellow Oxide.

14 Finishing Apply 2-3 coats of satin varnish.

French style wardrobe

I gave a new lease of life to a dowdy, secondhand wardrobe which I bought in a market. I just sanded back the surface using a fine grade of paper to cut back the varnish. In the old days, some pigments faded and gave the look of separated shades of colour. Varnishes tend to go yellow and milky with age and the technique illustrated here emulates this effect.

Only individual components of the wardrobe design are shown on the template as these elements can be combined in various ways to fit any surface. Just trace a few scrolls, cut out the tracings and arrange them to fit your wardrobe or chest of drawers. Tape them into position and retrace the overall pattern.

MATERIALS

Round brushes No. 4, 6

8 cm/3 in. sponge brush

Marine sponge

Art carbon

Stylus

Tracing paper

Low tack tape

Tack cloth

Crackle glaze

Satin varnish

Satin spray varnish/oil-based varnish

Colour palette

Alizarin Crimson

Regency Green

Antique White

Parisian Yellow

Hooker's Green

Antique Gold

Persian Rose

Olive Green

Raw Sienna

Yellow Oxide

Prussian Green artists' oil colour

Titanium White artists' oil colour

INSTRUCTIONS

1 **Background** With an 8 cm/3 in. sponge brush give the whole of the wardrobe a basecoat of Parisian Yellow, picking out any mouldings in Regency Green.

2 Use Antique Gold to accentuate any interesting features or mouldings. This colour should be done first as gold paints do not crackle. A distressed look can be given to the gold by sponging over with the same wash as the rest of the wardrobe.

3 Apply the crackle glaze to the surface of the wardrobe and when it is dry, sponge a wash of Antique White over the entire surface.

4 Once dry, mix a little Prussian Green artists' oil paint with enough white spirit to make a very thin wash and rub this over the entire surface using a soft cloth. Buff off the excess with a clean cloth. The green will stain the sponged white paint. Leave this to dry for a few hours. So little of this mix is left on the

surface that it will not affect the acrylic paint used for painting the design.

5   Transfer the design. If you want it to look deeply crazed, add a little more crackle glaze to the tips of the scrolls and under the roses before you start to paint.

6   **Scrolls**   Using a No. 6 round brush loaded with Yellow Oxide, paint the predominate part of the scroll by placing two comma strokes end to end. Add the fine lines and embellishments; accentuate with commas and 'S' strokes using Raw Sienna (see worksheet opposite).

7   **Leaves**   Load a No. 4 or a No. 6 round brush with a mix of equal parts of Hooker's Green and Olive Green, plus enough satin varnish or clear glazing medium to make the mix translucent. Paint in the leaves, using simple comma and 'S' strokes.

8   **Roses**   Give the roses a basecoat of the pale Persian Rose with the No. 4 round brush. Load the brush with pale rose pink then flatten and sideload with the dark Persian Rose (see page 26). Use the 'C' stroke with the darker shade pointing to the base of the rose, and shade the centre and base of the bowl. To paint the petals, load the brush with the pale mix of Persian Rose, then flatten and side load the brush with the dark Persian Rose (see page 26). Keeping the dark shade to the outer edges of the petals, define the back rows of petals using small comma strokes. Stipple the centres by loading the brush with orange made up of Yellow Oxide and Alizarin Crimson, kick loaded with Persian Rose. Use comma and wave strokes to define the outer petals and the bowl of the rose.

9   Erase all remaining tracing lines.

10   To give the wardrobe a soft, aged effect, mix the Titanium White artists' oil paint with the white spirit to a thin wash and wipe it over the whole surface of the wardrobe.

11   **Finishing**   Do not brush a water-based varnish over the project. This will soften the crackle glaze and ruin your work. Only very thin oil-based washes are used over the crackle glaze to stain it. This will not be enough to provide a protective coat as in proper antiquing. Either use an acrylic spray varnish or an oil-based varnish to seal the surface.

Antique chest

This chest was also inspired by my visit to Russia. It is relatively simple as it uses very basic techniques, but you do need a little patience. I am very pleased with the effect and hope you enjoy this project. The design template has been coded with the first letter of the colours to be used. To make it easier to follow, you might like to put dots of the required colours over the letters, as this makes it much quicker for the eye to see when referring to the design.

MATERIALS

Round brushes No. 2, 4

Flat brush No. 8

Liner brush No. 5/0

5 cm/2 in. sponge brush

000 fine steel wool

Coarse household brush

Varnishing brush

Art carbon

Tracing paper

Stylus

Low tack tape

Antiquing medium

Satin varnish

Colour palette

Yellow Oxide

Antique White

Burnt Umber

Raw Umber

Terracotta

Hooker's Green

Indigo

Burnt Umber artists' oil paint

INSTRUCTIONS

1 **Background** Make up a pale yellow mix of Antique White and Yellow Oxide. When painting the background colour on the box you can use a coarse brush to create the ridged effect in wood. This is particularly effective on MDF or any other kind of fibreboard which has a very smooth surface. The ridges will be accentuated when you come to the final antiquing stage.

2 Transfer the design leaving out the fine detail.

3 Block in the Indigo panels and the Raw Umber cross bands with a No. 8 flat brush.

4 When this is dry, transfer the details on both the Yellow and Indigo panels.

5 **Horses** Paint the horses with a No. 4 round brush loaded with Raw Umber. Outline and detail with Burnt Umber using a No. 2 round brush.

6 All the small embellishments are painted alternately in Terracotta and Hooker's Green using the No. 4 round brush.

7 When all these details have been painted, outline everything with Burnt Umber using a No. 2 round brush or 5/0 liner. The outlines and dots on the Indigo panels are Yellow Oxide.

8 **Finishing** Use 000 steel wool to distress the chest around the corners and areas that would have taken the most wear and tear. Antique with Burnt Umber artists' oil paint and then satin varnish.

Design Templates

The 20 design templates illustrated in this section can be reduced or enlarged on a photocopier to the appropriate size to fit the piece you are painting. Once you have done this, trace the design straight on to the surface (see page 13).

BLUE AND WHITE TULIP TABLE

SUNFLOWER PLATTER

DAISY CHAIR

ROSE MAGAZINE RACK

ROSE MAGAZINE RACK

FLOWERS ON A WALL CLOCK

COCKEREL PLAQUE

PANSY HAT BOX

POPPY BREAD BIN

LION BOOK BOX

SCROLL WASTEBIN

I INDIGO
O OLIVE GREEN
T TERRACOTTA

BLACKBERRY BREADBOARD

NAÏVE CLOCK

NAUTICAL LAP DESK

NAUTICAL LAP DESK

ROSE AND TULIP TRAY

FRUIT BASKET ON CABINET

FRUIT BASKET ON CABINET

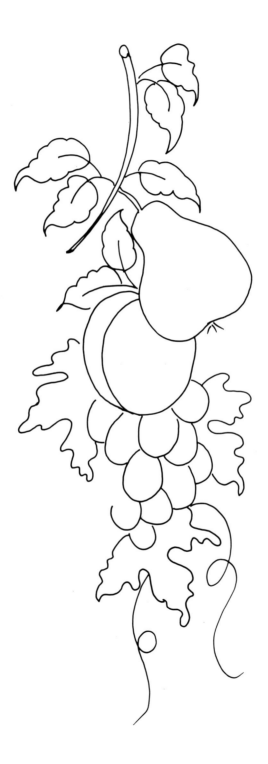

LACE BOOK BOX

ROSES AND RIBBON CHAIR

SPRING FLOWER MIRROR

SPRING FLOWER MIRROR

FRENCH STYLE WARDROBE

ANTIQUE CHEST

ANTIQUE CHEST

O DOTS OF YELLOW OXIDE
T TERRACOTTA
I INDIGO
H HOOKER'S GREEN
R RAW UMBER
Y YELLOW OXIDE

BRUSHSTROKE PRACTISE SHEET

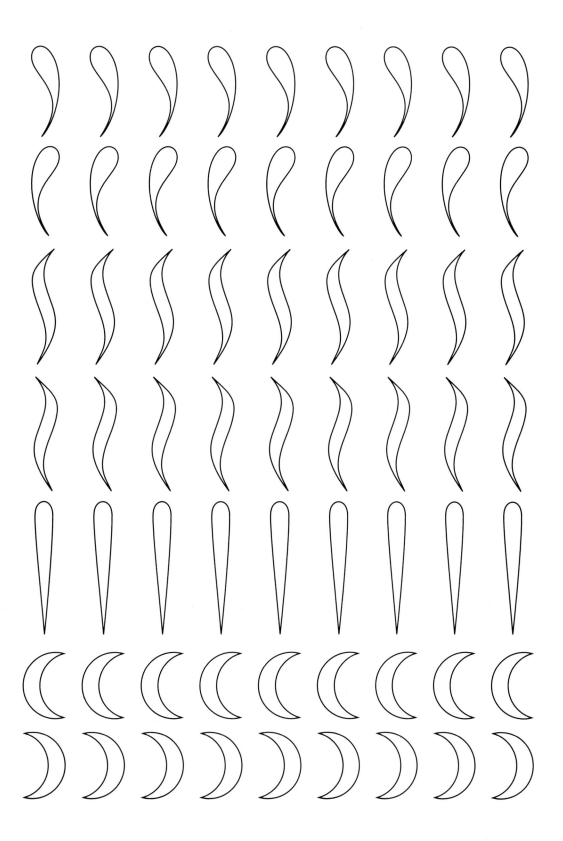

List of Suppliers

UK

The Decorative Arts Co.*
(courses, paints and blanks)
5a Royal Crescent
London W11 4SL
0171 371 4303
www.classicengland.co.uk/
design/decorate/decor05.html

Ashtree
*(lining paste, glazes,
specialist brushes, paints)*
Unit 37H
Mildmay Grove
London N1 4RH
0171 359 4696

Belinda Ballantine
*(small pots emulsion, crackle
varnish, specialist brushes
and blanks)*
The Abbey Brewery
Malmesbury
Wiltshire SN16 9AS
01666 822047

Mrs Casselden
(teaching and supplies)
159 Westminster Road
Sutton
Surrey SM1 3NQ
0181 641 4007

Cornelissen and Son Ltd
*(artists' and gilding
materials, paints,
liquid gum arabic)*
105 Great Russell Street
London WC1B 3RY
0171 636 1045

Green and Stone
*(artists' and gilding
materials)*
259 King's Road
London SW3 5EL
0171 352 0837

Janik Ltd*
(blanks)
Brickfield Lane
Ruthin
Denbighshire LL15 2TN
01824 702096

London Graphic Centre
*(general range of artists'
supplies and paints)*
16-18 Shelton Street
London WC2H 9JJ
0171 240 0095

John Myland Ltd
*(waxes, shellac, sanding
sealer, white polish)*
80 Norwood High Street
London SE27 9NW
0181 670 9161

Paint Magic*
(specialist paints, blanks)
79 Shepperton Road
London N1 3DF
0171 354 9696

Paper and Paints Ltd
*(historic paint colours,
artists' materials,
finishing brushes)*
4 Park Walk
London SW10 OAD
0171 352 8626

E Ploton *(Sundries)* **Ltd**
*(Artists' and gilding
materials, sanding sealer,
shellac and white polish)*
273 Archway Road
London N6 5AA
0181 348 0315

Polyvine Ltd
*(water-based sealers,
varnishes, glazes, stains and
paints)*
Vine House
Rockhampton
Berkley
Gloucestershire GL13 9DT
01454 261276

Scumble Goosie*
(blanks)
Lewiston Mill
Toadsmoor Road
Stroud
Gloucestershire GL5 2TB
01453 731305

Stuart R Stevenson
*(brushes, artists' and gilding
materials)*
68 Clerkenwell Road
London EC1M 5QA
0171 253 1693

Westcountry Finishes Ltd
*(water-based sealers,
varnishes, stains and paints)*
Unit 4
Station Business Park
Lower Brinley Ind. Estate
Teignmouth
Devon TQ14 8QJ
01626 779 994

Ann Witchell
(teaching and supplies)
5 Cowley Way
Sutton Benger
Chippenham SN15 1SD

USA

**Society of Decorative
Painters**
393 N. McLean Blvd
Wichita
Kansas KS 67203

The Artists' Club*
5750 NE Hassalo
Building C
Portland
Oregon 97213
(800) 845 6507

Cabin Craft Midwest*
1225 West 1st Street
Nevada
Iowa 50201
(800) 669 3920

Char-Lee Originals*
PO Box 606
Somonauk
Illinois 6055
(800) 242 7533

AUSTRALIA

Sue Schirmer
Victorian Academy of
Decorative Art
369 Camberwell Road
Camberwell
Melbourne
Victoria 3124

Elsa's Folk Art Studio
12 Myrtle Street
Normanhurst
Sydney
NSW 2076

The Folk Art Studio
200 Pittwater Road
Manly
Sydney
NSW 2095

* Mail order service

Index

antique chest 114, 139, 140

antiquing 16-17

art carbon 10

basecoat 13

blackberry breadboard 74, 127

blocking in 14

blue and white tulip table 38, 116

brushes

care of 9

types of 8-9

brushstrokes 20-29

'C' 22

comma 21

exclamation 22

fan 24

mistakes 29

practice sheet 141

ruffle 27

'S' 21

wave 23

cockerel plaque 56, 122

colour

choice of 18

recipes 19

crackling

glaze 17

varnish 17-18

cross hatching 14

daisy chair 46, 118

design

templates 116-140

tips 13

transferring 13-14

dry brush technique 14

floating colour 15

flowers on a wall clock 52, 121

fly specking 14

French style wardrobe 110, 138

fruit basket on cabinet 92, 132, 133

glaze 15

history 5

lace book box 96, 134

lion book box 70, 125

liquid masking 10

loading

back load 25

double side load 28

flatten and side load 26-27

kick load 26

liner brush load 23

round brush load 20, 24

side load 28

side tip load 25

tip load 24

triple load and blend 29

marbling 18

mistakes 15, 29

naïve clock 78, 128

nautical lap desk 82, 129, 130

paint

acrylic 8

colour recipes 19

effects 16-18

techniques 14-15

pansy hat box 60, 123

poppy bread bin 64, 124

push/pull technique 14-15

retarder 10, 15

rose and tulip tray 88, 131

rose magazine rack 48, 119, 120

roses and ribbon chair 100, 135

sanding sealer 11

scroll wastebin 72, 126

shading 15

shellac 11

sponging 16

Spring flower mirror 104, 136, 137

staining 13

steel wool 11

stippling 16

stylus 11

sunflower platter 42, 117

surface preparation 12-13

tack cloth 11

templates 116-140

tinting 15

varnish

crackle 17-18

oil-based 11

water-based 11

washes 15

white polish 11